John Plummer

Songs of Labour

Northamptonshire Rambles and other Poems

John Plummer

Songs of Labour
Northamptonshire Rambles and other Poems

ISBN/EAN: 9783744775823

Printed in Europe, USA, Canada, Australia, Japan

Cover: Foto ©Thomas Meinert / pixelio.de

More available books at **www.hansebooks.com**

SONGS OF LABOUR,

NORTHAMPTONSHIRE RAMBLES,

AND OTHER

POEMS.

BY JOHN PLUMMER.

LONDON:

W. TWEEDIE, 337, STRAND, W.C.

KETTERING: THOMAS WADDINGTON, HIGH STREET.

1860.

TO

THE RIGHT HONOURABLE

HENRY, LORD BROUGHAM AND VAUX;

THE TRUE AND FEARLESS EXPONENT

OF

THE RIGHTS, DUTIES, AND DIGNITY OF LABOUR;

THIS LITTLE VOLUME,

THE OFFSPRING OF THE LEISURE MOMENTS

OF

A FACTORY OPERATIVE,

IS RESPECTFULLY DEDICATED,

AS A HUMBLE TOKEN

OF

SINCERE GRATITUDE,

BY THE AUTHOR.

PREFACE.

HAD the Author merely consulted his own desires, he would have refrained from the publication of the present collection; for he is fully conscious of the numerous faults which abound in it: but having yielded to the earnest solicitation of those whose friendship has lightened many a long weary hour of toil and anxiety, he has collected, in their present shape, many of his compositions which, until lately, have been leading a fugitive existence in the "Poet's Corner" of various provincial periodicals and newspapers.

He is quite aware that he must not look for mercy from the generality of critics; but he would respectfully beg of them to consider the circumstances under which his pieces were composed, and to reflect that, if they do not betray the promise of a Keats, or of a Massey, still, they are the offspring of a true and earnest aspiration for better things.

Many of them were written at a period when unreflective and impulsive passion, rather than the softening and humanizing dictates of judgment and reason, swayed the thoughts of the Author: yet, to quote the words of one, who, with an indomitable amount of power, talent, and genius, has passed through the same fiery ordeal of poverty, neglect, and suffering—GERALD MASSEY—"I retain my verses as memorials of my past, as one might keep some worn-out garment because he has passed through the furnace in it, nothing doubting that in the future they will often prove my passport to the hearts and homes of thousands of the poor.   *   *   *   *   *   They will know that I have suffered their suffering, wept their tears, thought their thoughts, and felt their feelings; and they will trust me."

AN AUTOBIOGRAPHICAL SKETCH

OF THE

AUTHOR'S LIFE.

It has become a custom, though perhaps not a very commendable one, to preface the works of those who have attracted any share, however limited, of the public attention, with some description of their career, so that the lessons of their struggles, success, or failure, may serve as finger posts to direct future wayfarers on the long, uphill, and ofttimes fatal, path of literature.

It is not from any feelings of vanity, or the promptings of an egotistical nature, which has induced me to comply with the wishes of many of the subscribers to the present volume, by prefixing a short personal memoir to its contents; but because it may be that the simple statement of my struggles against the force of adverse circumstances, may encourage those who, similarly afflicted with the infirmity under which I have so long laboured, have renounced all hope, and feel inclined to murmur at the will of Him, whose works prove that He ever ordains all things for our welfare and happiness.

There is scarcely a human being from whose history we may not gather some instructive lesson, which will serve

"To point a moral, or adorn a tale;"

and therefore I trust my readers will bear kindly with me, and forget the *critic* in the *man*, when judging of the merits of my rude attempts.

Near to the Tower of London, exists a neighbourhood unequalled for squalidness, poverty, and misery. I refer to the purlieus of Royal Mint Street, as it is now ambitiously designated, but which is better known by its ancient title of Rosemary Lane, although it is many, very many, years since it deserved a name which awakens the thoughts of sunny orchards, green meadows, and all the glorious beauty of nature. Old clothes' shops, kept by persons of unmistakably Jewish extraction; dirty low places, by courtesy termed "grocery stores"; milkshops, potatoe sheds, and flaunting handsome "gin palaces," line the main street, which forms the chief artery of a labyrinth of long, narrow, filthy courts, inhabited by Irish labourers, and the lowest and most poverty stricken of the London poor; and where scenes are daily, nay, hourly, enacted, which are sufficient to "make the Angels weep"; and to mock the proud boast of our vaunted progress in the path of civilization.

In this locality I was born, on the 3rd of June, 1831; my father being a staymaker in a small way of business for himself. Of my infancy, I can but glean few particulars; but I was always considered a very precocious child, and passionately fond of pictures and books. My father's trade was not very profitable; and when I was five years of age a serious illness overtook him, which prevented him from attending to his business, thereby deranging his affairs, and breaking up his little connexion. By this blow, the family were reduced to a state of the greatest distress; and I was sent to St. Albans, where an uncle took charge of me for awhile, so that I should not be a burden on the efforts of my parents, who struggled, but, alas! in vain, to recover their former position; and were compelled to accept of the kindness of my grandmother, who kindly offered them an attic in a house, of which she had the sole charge. To add to their difficulties, my poor mother had the misfortune to fracture her leg by a fall, and was never afterwards enabled to leave the house, except on a very few special occasions, until the time of her death at Kettering; while at the same time my infant bro-

ther, Edmund, died ; but, before his death, he was
continually expressing a wish to see me ; so I was
sent from St. Albans in charge of the carrier, but my
arrival was too late, for poor Edmund was no more.
I have but a dim perception of what followed, for
I can only recollect attending a funeral, and crying
bitterly ; as, immediately afterwards, all became a
total blank, till I found myself slowly recovering—
as from the dead—from the effects of a severe
fever.   When I began to recover my consciousness,
I was surprised at the stillness which seemed to
pervade the room.   My parents were moving about,
but I could not hear them ; and, although they
came to me, and moved their lips, yet I could not
hear them—*I was deaf !*   I tried to move, and to
sit up in bed, but my limbs refused their office—
I was lame ! besides being deaf.   The full extent
of my affliction remained unfelt by me at first ; and
it was not till long, long months of bitter suffering
had passed away, that I felt how my infirmities had
deprived me of the enjoyment of all that is sweet
and pleasing in the world of sound.   Years afterwards, when I discovered that I could pen what
some have pleased to term "poetry," I expressed
my feelings in the following lines, suggested by
Gerald Massey's touching lines—" 'Tis hard, 'tis
hard, to wander on through this bright world of
ours."

'Tis hard indeed for me to bear
   This wild and cruel fate—
To wander through this world of joy,
   Alone and desolate !
Nor hear the music of the wood—
   The warblings 'mid the tree ;
Nor all the pleasant sounds that float
   Upon the summer breeze.

To see the laughing infant leap
   At the maternal voice ;
To view the blushing maiden smile
   At tones that her rejoice ;
To mark the bright and flashing eyes
   Which glow at music's strain :
These bid my heart with anguish weep,
   Yet weep—alas !—in vain.

'Tis true I see the golden charms
   Which crown the brow of day ;
The shady woods, the sunny fields,
   With flowers bright and gay ;
Or else peruse the varied works
   Of minds that never die :
Yet still I ever yearn to hear
   The voice of sympathy.

For what is earth without the joys
   Friendship alone may give ?
A dreary, dark, and trackless waste,
   In which no heart may live !

The bravest soul—uncheer'd by hope—
    Will faint and weary prove,
If friendless—lonely—unsustain'd—
    It hears no voice of love.

About this time, my father obtained a situation as foreman in a stay factory in the city; and a small two-roomed house was taken by him in a poor and miserable locality, near Whitechapel, to which the family removed. Here I slowly recovered, to a great extent, the use of my limbs, and could walk about with comparative ease; and the intensity of my deafness was considerably modified, so that I could hear with less difficulty than had previously been experienced. To aid in eking out the limited means of the family, my mother began to commence business as a *middlewoman*, that is, one who obtains work, at a certain price, from the London warehouses, and gives it out to other workpeople at a less rate; the difference in the prices constituting her profits, which were scanty enough in all conscience. Being able to go about, as I was now about twelve years of age, I was sent out with portions of the work to the various workpeople who resided in the wretched, crime and fever reeking localities of Shadwell, Ratcliffe, Whitechapel, and Bethnal Green. While on these errands, I witnessed such scenes of vice, poverty, and suffering, as would rival, if not surpass, the wildest inventions of fiction ; and which I hope, some day, to embody in a work treating of such things.

Up to this time I had received no education, save what I may have obtained from the doubtful instruction of an old lady, whose chief care was to keep me quiet, rather than teach me anything ; but I always felt a strange kind of fascination for books ; and although I could not read them, yet I would pore for hours over the—to me—mystical letters of the alphabet. How I acquired the art of reading I cannot remember; for it was a very slow and gradual process, as I had no teachers, and my parents did not possess much more education than was possessed by the generality of their class : but I can remember striving to make out the words on the advertising placards so liberally posted on the street hoardings, and of studying the names placed at the ends of the streets : but the great impetus was given to my mind, when some stray copies of *The Penny Magazine*, *Lloyd's Penny Sunday Times*, and other illustrated periodicals of a similar nature, fell into my hands. No miser ever hugged his gold with a more jealous care, than I did the few old torn and soiled numbers which came into my possession. For hours I would gaze on the woodcuts, and strive to decipher the letter press descriptions, in which I at last succeeded; but I had no teachers, and no books of instruction, so that my self-culture was attended with extreme difficulty.

It would be too long a task to relate my numerous attempts to procure the books which my parents were too poor to purchase for me; or of my haunting the street bookstalls, where I gazed with sad, longing, and despairing, features on the literary treasures displayed before me, and which the want of a few pence alone precluded me from possessing. Sometimes I would take up a book, read a few pages; returning the next evening to read a few more, until at last I mastered the book. Once, however, after having thus perused part of a History of England, I was struck with consternation at missing the volume, which had been sold during my absence. I had never dreamt of the possibility of such an event; and my looks attracted the attention of the stall-keeper, who seemed intuitively to guess the cause of my trouble; and, as he was aware of my deafness, he wrote on a piece of paper, that he was sorry for my disappointment, but that I was welcome to peruse any of the books on his stall. Of course I was glad enough to avail myself of the opportunity thus afforded me, but I seldom had much time for that purpose. My father possessed a copy of Bunyan's Holy War, which, with an old edition of Robinson Crusoe, were read by me over and over again ; but I was always obliged to skip over the hard words.

Books ! books ! books ! was my continual cry ; and whether they were old Almanacks, Religious Tracts, Penny Story Books, or anything else, they were ever welcome : and I was always begging or borrowing them of the neighbours : and naturally so, for they enabled me, for the time, to forget my affliction, and converse, as it were, with the authors whose works came under my notice.

Time passed on, and I became more proficient in my studies, which were carried on under great disadvantages, because, as if my own infirmities were not obstacles enough, several of the workpeople persuaded my mother that my devotion to books would render me crazy, a statement which had the effect of occasioning her to forbid my reading any ; but I could not restrain my love for them, and I therefore kept one or two of them in my breeches pocket, so that I might secretly read them. Indeed my early life was one long, bitter time of wretchedness, occasioned by neglect, censure of my *supposed* dulness, and the ridicule and tormentings of my playmates, who were never weary of mimicking my deafness, and of playing every imaginable

trick on me. Every misdeed was laid on my
shoulders, and I was frequently punished for the
faults of others, till I became subject to fits of alter-
nate passion and despondency, which, however, frequently gave way to a natural buoyancy of spirits.
The knowledge of the injustice with which I was so
repeatedly treated, awakened in my breast a desire
to distinguish myself in some way, so that I might
prove that I was not the dunce, or incapable, which
I was supposed to be; and it was not long before
the opportunity arrived.

My father's position appeared to improve; and as
our prospects began to brighten, a larger house in
the neighbourhood was taken, and my father again
commenced business on his own account. I was
employed by him as errand boy, to assist in the
workshop, and make myself generally useful. Much
of my time was necessarily passed in the streets;
and, having a quick and observant eye, I soon made
myself familiar with all the phases of street life, so
graphically described by Henry Mayhew, in his
"*London Labour and the London Poor.*" I seldom
loitered on my errands, except when passing the
printsellers' shops near the Royal Exchange; my
duties frequently leading me to all parts of the
City, and to many districts of the West End; for
the works of pictorial art possessed even more

attractions for me than the charms of reading, and
it was with difficulty that I could restrain myself
from gazing on them for hours, as they were displayed in the windows. This feeling was stimulated
by the perusal of the lives of Painters in *The Penny
Magazine,* and *Chambers's Miscellany,* till at last
I resolved to enter the Spitalfield's School of Design
as an evening student. This was the only school of
any kind at which I attended ; and, at first, my
reception was of a nature enough to discourage a
less earnest student. Weary, unwashed, and
heated with the day's toil, I would arrive in time
for the evening classes, in spite of the sneers and
ridicule of many of the students, who beheld in my
awkwardness, and seeming stupidity, a target for
their witticisms and practical jokes. This fired my
soul ; and although I could scarcely write my
name on entering the school, yet, in nine months
time, I carried off the first prize for the best outline
drawing from the flat. Oh ! it was a proud day for
me, when Earl Granville gave me the prize at
Crosby Hall, in the presence of my former tormentors. Trifling as it was in itself, yet the mere
fact that I had beat them gave me fresh courage ;
and, by dint of perseverance, I soon found myself
in the head class, mastering perspective, mechanical
drawing, oil colour painting, painting in distemper,

&c., and gaining a first-class prize for an ornamental design. Those evenings were the happiest of my life, and I often recall, with a sigh of regret, the period of my art studies.

About this time (1848) the French Revolution occurred, and I shared in the general excitement consequent on its accomplishment. This naturally led me to peruse the newspapers, and to imbibe a powerful feeling in favour of revolutionary ideas ; but as the brilliant dreams of freedom faded one by one beneath the grasp of military despotism, I began to reflect on the causes of such results, and thus commenced those habits of thought and reasoning, which afterwards led me to become a humble disciple of that school which the names of Adam Smith, Brougham, Mill, Martineau, Bastiat, Ellis, Ricardo, &c., have rendered so illustrious.

About the same period I first became a victim to a taste for versifying, an art for which I had previously felt but slight inclination. How it came about was in the following wise. After the rebellion in Hungary was subdued through the treachery of Georgey, the English people waited with an impatient feeling the arrival of Kossuth, so that they might testify their sympathy for him, and also their approval of his efforts to obtain the blessings of freedom for his country. Like the rest of my class,

I was intensely excited, and longed to behold the man whom my feelings had led me to exalt in my mind as a godlike hero. I felt a yearning within me which sought an utterance in burning words of living welcome to the Hungarian exile. Prose seemed so stiff and solemn, that I desired something more in unison with the fierce leapings of my heart; but I longed in vain, till one day, as I was carrying a parcel down Fleet Street, I passed a little Chartist bookshop, near Fetter Lane, and, on looking at the window, I perceived a paper of verses, entitled " A Song of Welcome to Kossuth," by Gerald Massey.* Eureka! Oh! how the words danced about in my memory :—

" We meet him here, we greet him here;
    With Love's wide arms caress him;
And kings have no such welcome dear,
    As Kossuth hath, GOD BLESS HIM!"

From that time henceforth I idolized Song as the truest exponent of man's deepest feelings; and although, since then, I have changed many of my old opinions, and learned to gaze with a calmer eye on the ever shifting scenes of Continental politics; yet never till my dying hour shall I forget the glorious enthusiasm of that moment, when a new and heavenly existence seemed opened up before me.

* This was before his Poems were published by Bogue.

That my verses are poor, weak, and ofttimes devoid
originality, I fully admit; but that fact does not
prevent me from appreciating the utterances of
those whose works I may never hope or dare to
emulate; and despite its faults, which were produced by the conditions of his life, I deem the
poetry of Gerald Massey to be the most in accord-
ance with the general tone of opinion entertained by
the majority of working men of the present day.
My leisure time was now divided between studying
at the School of Design and scribbling verses in
secret; but my effusions were very poor indeed,
and I felt them to be so, therefore I refrained from
imitating the example of many of my betters, and
did *not* plague the editors of periodicals with forlorn requests "to peruse, and, if possible, insert
them in their pages;" an act of self-denial which
has spared me much remorse, which I should otherwise have experienced at the present time, for the
sufferings occasioned to the poor unoffending editors.

But a circle of misfortune was drawn rapidly
around the family; and after many vain attempts
to retrieve his position, my father sought for employment, and obtained his present situation, in a
stay factory at Kettering. My poor mother had
been seized with a serious illness, from which she
never recovered, although the journey to Kettering

appeared at first to do her some little good. I was compelled to give up all hopes of prosecuting my art studies, as I, otherwise, had no means of obtaining a livelihood for some time. It was with the deepest regret that I abandoned my dreams of an artistic life, to exchange the pencil for the shears, and the drawing board for the cutting table; but who can resist the stern decrees of fate? for what *will* be, *must* be. Therefore, with a heavy heart and ruined hopes, I left the Metropolis, to enter on my fresh sphere of labour. I here ought to mention an act of kindness on the part of my former master at the School of Design, Mr. John Walsh, then Professor of Anatomy at Marlborough House. He applied to Mr. Henry Cole, of the Science and Art department, and obtained permission for me to continue my studies free of all charge; but, unfortunately, having no friends to aid me in my penniless condition, and my infirmity closing many employments of a remunerative nature against me, I was compelled to decline an offer so honorable to those who proposed it. From that time my art studies have totally ceased; but I have preserved, with a religious care, the majority of my drawings and designs. I came to Kettering, and obtained my present situation in the stay factory. This was towards the close of 1853. In

1854 my mother, who had for several months been afflicted with a mortal disorder, became much worse, and many a night, when I returned from my work, I had to sit up attending on her, so that a little rest might be obtained by my sister; but all our efforts proved unavailing, and before long we had to mourn the loss of one who was truly in every sense a good wife and a tender mother.

The numerous troubles which had so rapidly succeeded each other, involved the family in serious pecuniary difficulties, from which there was great trouble in extricating ourselves, despite the many efforts made by some of us; and I could perceive no way of gratifying my artistic yearnings or literary predilections, until, in 1855, when the newspaper stamp was abolished. In that year a cheap penny paper was started at Kettering, partly printed there, and partly in London, under the name of "Charles Knight's Town and Country Newspaper." An offer was made to me to act as local reporter; but, though my deafness had so far improved that I could hold conversation with persons close to me, I could not then, nor at present, hear the speeches at meetings distinctly enough to report them, consequently I was obliged to decline it. I have had many similar offers within the last few months, but have had to refuse them all for the same reason. However, it was intimated to me that literary contributions on local topics would be very acceptable ; and as I foresaw in the offer an opportunity of familiarizing myself with newspaper writing I cheerfully spent much of my leisure time in composition, and studying the questions treated. My range of subjects was a rather varied one, for it embraced every possible topic of the day. Letters and articles on Capital Punishment ; Parliamentary Representation ; The Maine Law ; Peace ; The Russian War ; Reading Rooms; Reviews of Longfellow, Mrs. Browning, &c. ; Constantinople ; Dear Bread ; English Poisoning ; Slavery ; Reminiscences of London ; Chartism ; The Labour Question ; The Future of France ; Temperance ; America ; Austria and Italy ; Machinery ; Religious Awakening ; Electro-biology ; Penny Banks ; The Health of Towns' Act, &c., &c. ; besides numberless pieces of verse, were contributed by me to the columns of the paper mentioned ; and their appearance occasioned me to extend my circle of writing, especially within the last two years ; so that, at the time I pen this crude sketch, I find that nearly 1,500 letters, essays, poems, paragraphs, &c., have appeared from my pen in various newspapers : but of course as my work was not done for remuneration I scarcely received any, although

I have formed several valued intimacies with members of the press. The first thing which drew my name into public note was a hot controversy with the Roman Catholic Canon of Northampton—the Rev. John Dalton—on various things relating to his religion; and in which I was led to use an acerbity which I now regret. So things went on until the winter of 1857-58, when the factory was closed for several weeks, and I was deprived of employment, with but slender resources of my own to subsist on. Taking advantage of a cheap railway excursion, I went to London in search of employment; failing in which, and losing my railway return ticket, I had to walk from Hitchin to Kettering, a distance of 45 miles, in one day. The weather was cold, the snow fell heavily, and my crippled knee was so sore and stiff with pain that I became utterly hopeless, and could not help breathing the lines of Massey's "Cry of the Unemployed."—

> "I'd work but cannot, starve I may, but will not beg
>   for bread:
> God of the wretched, hear my prayer; I WOULD
>   THAT I WERE DEAD."

However, the sunny days of Spring came, bringing with them employment, and new born hopes of the future; and I proceeded with redoubled vigour, under every possible disadvantage, to devote my little leisure to literary pursuits.

But my brother, being discontented at the dreary prospects of the stay trade, (he worked with me and my father in the stay factory,) resolved to become a shoe maker. Now, it so happened that the shoe makers of Northampton were engaged in a "strike" against the introduction of machinery into the trade, and had formed a powerful organization, with branches in various parts of the county. In their code of rules, they declared that—"It is high time that the employed should have a fair share of the benefits arising from the productive industry of the country, as well as the employer, and not to be obliged in his old age to finish a life of labour in a poor-law bastile, and a pauper's grave, while those for whom he has toiled hard, are allowed to revel in luxury, through their assumed rights to dictate their own terms to the workman, and the carrying out of their favorite dogma of unrestricted competition." Well, Japheth little thought that, in denouncing the tyranny of the masters, the men were setting up a despotism of their own ; therefore he "applied to a shoe maker, one of the members of the committee, who agreed to teach him on the receipt of a certain amount as remuneration ; but *after* the agreement, and *before* my brother went to learn, the Kettering branch passed a bye-law to the effect that no one should be allowed to learn the art of shoe making after he had attained the age of 17, nor without giving a sufficient remuneration to the teacher; and that no shoe maker should have, at any one time, more than two apprentices. On this, the person who had engaged to teach him, declined doing so; he therefore applied to another man, (not belonging to the society,) but this person was deterred by threats from teaching him; so he determined to teach himself, and so far succeeded that he was able to obtain employment from a wholesale firm in the trade. But the Kettering executive sent a deputation to wait on the masters, to inform them that if they continued to employ Japheth Plummer, they would strike the shop. Of course, at the busy time when this occurred, the employers were reluctantly obliged to refrain from employing him." This led me to publish some letters on his behalf in a local paper, in which I defended "The Rights of Labour," and attacked the Shoe Makers' Union by every possible argument. But, after awhile, my letters were refused admission by the editor, who feared lest he should incur the displeasure of the Union, and lose his subscribers. Nothing daunted, I set to work to pen a pamphlet; but as I did not possess the means of printing it, my brother and I canvassed several of the shoe manufacturers at Northampton,* and obtained orders for a number of copies sufficient to defray all the printing expenses, so that I was enabled to publish it.

On the appearance of the *Freedom of Labour*,† a copy was sent to Lord Brougham, with a request to allow the second edition to be dedicated to him, which favour was courteously conceded.

It would be an invidious task to summarize my

* A History of the Strike at Northampton is published in the REPORT OF THE TRADES' UNION COMMITTEE OF THE SOCIAL SCIENCE ASSOCIATION. London: J. W. Parker.

† I must here perform an act of justice to Mr. Charles Knight. In three of my tracts there appear some quotations from "The Results of Machinery," and "The Rights of Industry," which I have, by mistake, attributed to Lord Brougham instead of Mr. Knight. It is but fair to state that his lordship disclaimed the authorship of the treatises. Mr. Knight's works originally appeared twenty years ago, but without his name being attached; and as they were published under the sanction of the Society for the Diffusion of Useful Knowledge, they were, and still are, by many persons, attributed to Lord Brougham. In THE WEEKLY VOLUME and KNOWLEDGE IS POWER, Mr. Knight avowed the authorship of the treatises, but the former had escaped my memory, and the latter I had not seen, hence the mistake, which, however, is highly flattering to Mr. Knight.

career from this point, therefore an extract from the
Northampton Herald of January 14th, 1860, must
conclude this brief sketch of a working man's life—

"The tract was favourably mentioned by Lord
Brougham in his celebrated Liverpool speech on
Popular Education, and was speedily followed by
another on Strikes ; but all this only increased the
ferment against the Plummers.   John was burnt in
effigy, his infirmity cruelly caricatured, and his
life threatened, while his brother lost much time
and money in prosecuting some of his tormentors ;
but, after awhile, their efforts were successful, and
John beheld the complete triumph of the principles
advocated by him.   This naturally led his attention
to the builders' strike in London, and caused him
to publish a tract on the subject, which procured
him the notice of Lord Brougham in the House of
Lords,* and also the approbation of many eminent

---

* On the opening of the Liverpool Free Library and Museum, October 17th, 1860, his Lordship was pleased to again
notice my slight efforts in the following words :—

" I have another working man to cite, in consequence of having
received this morning a document, as if the author had had a
presentiment that I was about to attend a meeting of working
men.   I allude now to a working man who has distinguished
himself, not in mechanism, but in a subject of a higher order than
working men generally enter into—I mean a most excellent
address, well reasoned, upon a most important subject, namely,

authorities, such as John Stuart Mill, T. Buckle, Leoni Levi, G. Godwin, W. Ellis, W. B. Hodgson, L.L.D., C. Neate, M.A., G. Pryne, M.A., Jacob Waley, M.A., T. E. Cliffe Leslie, L.L D., &c., &c. All the while, however, he has quietly followed his employment as a cutter of stays, by the aid of steam machinery, in a factory at Kettering, ; and as his hours of employment are from 8 a.m. to 8 p.m., it seems somewhat incomprehensible how he could manage to write the numerous poems, essays, tales, letters, &c.—570 in number[*]—which he has contributed to the "Builder," "Building News," "Cassell's Paper," "Family Herald," "Weekly

that of strikes, referred to by Mr. Brown. Upon this subject great mistakes have been committed by some who have been setting labour against capital, as if capital were the enemy of labour. Such doctrines are apt to injure the men who put them forth far more than their employers. I allude to John Plummer, whom two years ago I had to quote for another pamphlet he wrote. This man is a working staymaker of Kettering, Northamptonshire, and he has just published an address to the working men of Yorkshire to dissuade them from any such injurious, and at times most costly, proceedings as those of setting up labour in opposition to the capital employed. (Cheers) I can only say of one of these tracts, that no man could reason the subject better, and shall say the same of the present; and I hope and trust that my old friends and constituents of Yorkshire will give a serious and calm attention to Mr. Plummer's reasoning."

* Now nearly 1500 in number.

Record," "London News," "Christian Cabinet," "Advertiser," "Scottish Journal," and many others; besides a new tract on Trades' Unions, dedicated to the Earl of Shaftesbury, and highly approved of by Lord St. Leonards, and other gentlemen; a paper on Strikes, for the Social Science Association; a prize essay on Sanitary Reform, &c. He has received many presents of books from various distinguished persons; and very recently the Rev. Sir G. S. Robinson spoke very highly of him at a public dinner.* Ever industrious, Mr. Plummer carries on a continual and extensive correspondence with many of the leading minds of the kingdom, and it was the knowledge of this fact which induced Lord Palmerston to grant him £40 from Her Majesty's royal bounty. It is Mr. Plum-

---

* "I am happy to say that amongst our artizans are to be found many intelligent men, who are an honour to their country, * * * * I know one such man as those to whom I have alluded. I have on my lips one name—the name of an honest and intelligent man, who has laboured hard to enlighten his fellow-workmen on such questions as these. He has laboured hard here and elsewhere. I allude to John Plummer, of Kettering, whom I know to be an honest man, and who has had the courage to tell his fellow-workmen the truth. It is the labours of such men that I look forward for great things to come."...NORTHAMPTON HERALD, October 1st, 1859.

mer's earnest desire to publish a volume of poems, but, although the encouragement he has received is of a most highly-flattering nature, he shrinks from the expense in which it would involve him; but should his dreams be realised, he may possibly be enabled, by means of the profits arising from its sale, to devote himself to those labours in which he has been so markedly successful, and which, but for his infirmities, would have long since placed him in a very advantageous position. Few men in John Plummer's position in life can boast of so much effected with such limited means and numerous obstacles in so short a space of time; and it is to be hoped that he may find friends who will enable him to assume the position so ardently desired by him."

I cannot lay down my pen until I have expressed my sincerest thanks to those kind-hearted and generous minds—such as Lord Brougham, Lord Ashburton, Lord Palmerston, M. D. Hill, Esq., the Recorder of Birmingham, the Rev. G. E. Maunsell, of Thope Rectory, near Kettering, and many others—who, by presents of books, and other material aids, have very largely increased my means of usefulness; and should it ever please the Almighty that my sphere of usefulness be enlarged, so that I may devote more time to share, in common with numerous other lowly toilers in the good work, the high and noble task of inculcating the doctrines of Temperance, Prudence, Morality, and Education, amongst those of our fellow-workers, who so bitterly need such teachings, I fervently hope and trust that my works will NEVER belie the meed of approbation which they have hitherto received, and of which I am so proud, not because of my own sake, but for the sake of that order to which, by birth, education, and daily-life, I belong.

KETTERING, NOVEMBER, 1860.

INDEX.

SONGS OF LABOUR.

NORTHAMPTONSHIRE RAMBLES, &c.

MISCELLANEOUS POEMS.

SONGS OF LABOUR.

SONGS OF LABOUR,

&c., &c.

FAITH, HOPE, AND CHARITY.

Thou may'st be fair ; oh ! fair beyond
    The aid of Language to express ;
Thy cheek may bid the Rose despond,
    Or be the Lily's pale distress.
Yet these are worthless, if thy heart
    To gentle deeds a stranger be ;
Alas ! poor Maiden, if thou part
    From Faith, and Hope, and Charity.

Thou may'st be rich with worldly dross,
    Thy nod may cause a world to bow ;
Nor creature poor presume to cross
    The path of one so great as Thou !

B

Yet what avails thy fortune rare
    When Death's rude hand shall summons thee,
If thou—Proud Man—did'st never care
    For Faith, and Hope, and Charity?

Thou may'st be skill'd in Learning's lore,
    And seek to probe Man's secret dreams;
Or strive on Fancy's wings to soar
    To happier, holier, brighter themes.
Yet futile is thy toil to win
    The prize of Fame, and Love to thee,
If, in thy zeal, thou should'st but sin
    'Gainst Faith, and Hope, and Charity.

Hail! hallow'd Three, whose peaceful smile
    Can crown each soul with sweet delight—
Can ev'ry Care and Grief beguile
    With sweetest feelings, pure and bright.
Oh! Brothers come with kindly heart,
    And learn to own the angel Three;
Nor let your souls in sadness part
    From Faith, and Hope, and Charity.

HARVEST HOME.

In the dark Fog-days of the early year,
   When the Storm-blasts howl'd, and the Snow-
      flakes fell,
And the white Fields mourn'd in their loneness
      drear,
   While the bright Streams fled at the Ice-King's
      spell ;
Then the Seed lay bound in the cold hard ground,
   And the Hedgerows sigh'd with a cheerless moan,
While the bleak bare woods e'er rung with the sound
   Of Nature pleading at her tyrant's throne.
But the Winter passed, and the laughing Spring
   Bade the rich warm light of the Sunshine come ;
And the Farmer's voice with a joy would ring,
   As he dream'd with hope of the Harvest Home.
      Hurrah ! Hurrah ! for the laden Wain,
      Piled to the top with the golden Grain ;
      And Hurrah ! Hurrah ! for the men that come,
      And Hurrah ! Hurrah ! for the Harvest Home.

In the bright May morn, when the Lark sang high,
  And the Flowers peep'd forth from the Roadside
      green ;
While the soft south Winds from the groves swept by,
  To the far off Hills in the distance seen ;
In its glad young strength, up the Corn-blade
      sprung,
  And smil'd as it kiss'd, in the op'ning day,
All the shining drops of the Dew that hung
  On its trembling form, as a crystal spray.
And the Cotter rais'd, in a prayer, his voice,
  To the far star-worlds of the azure dome—
Where the Angels dwell, and the Blest rejoice—
  For success and joy to the Harvest Home.
        Hurrah ! Hurrah ! for the laden Wain,
        Piled to the top with the golden Grain ;
        And Hurrah! Hurrah! for the Men that come,
        And Hurrah! Hurrah! for the Harvest Home.

Soon the Reapers went in the early morn,
  While folks in their beds, in the dull Town lay ;
And before them fell all the rich ripe corn,
  Tied up in the sheaves by the Damsels gay.
And the Poor Man smiled as he heard them sing :
  He knew that his Babes would shout in their glee,
When he unto them should the cheap food bring,
  In its plenty rare, from the bread-tax free ;

While the Toilers pale, in the large towns drear—
  Where Vice, and Sorrow, and Wretchedness roam—
Felt the new-born hopes of the Future cheer
  Their hearts, as they thought of the Harvest Home.
      Hurrah ! Hurrah ! for the laden Wain,
      Piled to the top with the golden Grain ;
      And Hurrah ! Hurrah ! for the Men that come,
      And Hurrah ! Hurrah ! for the Harvest Home.

TIMOTHY BENNETT.

Timothy Bennett was a shoemaker at Hampton-Wick, in Surrey.
The first passage from this village to Kingston-on-Thames,
through Bushy Park, had for many years been shut up from
the public; but honest Tim, "unwilling," as he said, "to leave
the world worse than he found it," determined to recover it for
the use of his fellow-toilers; and, after a long series of efforts,
he succeeded in convincing Lord Halifax that he (the noble-
man) was WRONG, and that Timothy Bennett, the poor shoemaker, was RIGHT. The result was, that the public enjoy
the road to this day. Timothy died in 1756.

On ! true was his Soul and noble his Heart,
  Its Saxon pride evermore scorning
To act in its sphere the pale Coward's part,
  On Wealth and on Tyranny fawning.

" For in Life," said Tim, " shall this be my plan.
　　(And never shall Foeman confound it,)
To do in this world the best that I can,
　　Nor leave it still worse than I found it."

There's many a King, and many a Lord,
　　Would find that their rule was the lighter ;
And never need Gaoler, Scaffold, or Sword,
　　To render their Glory the brighter,
Did they but hearken to Timothy's plan,
　　Though troubles may seem to surround it,
And do in this world the best that they can,
　　Nor leave it still worse than they found it.

We've Sorrow and Anguish, Passion and Hate,
　　Our Hearts' better nature oft shrouding ;
We've Sin, Shame, and Hunger, lying in wait,
　　The sky of our Happiness clouding ;
And England has mourn'd for years the dark ban
　　Which silently hover'd around it,
Till warm hearts, like Tim's, slow followed his plan,
　　Nor left the world worse than they found it.

But never will we e'er yield to despair,
　　For better times hopelessly mourning ;
Never shall England her duty forswear,
　　The promise of brighter days scorning.

No ! still for the Truth we'll battle, each Man,
  And tear down the mists that surround it,
Teaching our brothers that Timothy's plan
  Ne'er left the World worse than it found it.

SMILE AND BE CONTENTED.

The World grows old, and Men grow cold
  To each whilst seeking Treasure ;
And what with Want, and Care, and Toil,
  We scarce have time for Pleasure :
But never mind, that is a loss
  Not much to be lamented ;
Life rolls on gaily if we will
  But Smile and be Contented.

If we are Poor and would be Rich,
  It will not be by pining ;
No ! steady Hearts and hopeful Minds
  Are Life's bright silver lining.
There's ne'er a man that dared to *hope*,
  Hath of his choice repented :
The happiest Souls on Earth are those
  Who Smile and are Contented.

When grief doth come to rack the Heart,
　　And fortune bids us sorrow,
From Hope we may a blessing reap
　　And consolation borrow.
If Thorns will rise where Roses bloom,
　　It cannot be prevented ;
So make the best of Life you can,
　　And Smile and be Contented.

THE MASON'S SONG.

Up, up with the Dawn
Of the bright glad Morn,
The Ladders high we climb ;
And the Trowels ring
As we work, and sing
Some good old English rhyme.

We slave in no room,
We pine at no Loom,
Where sick'ning Gas-lights glare ;
Where the poor Souls moil
And sigh at their toil,
Shut out from God's own air.

Oh ! our hearts are strong,
Our laugh loud and long,
With Care undimm'd our eyes,
As, block upon block,
And firm as a rock,
The Walls before us rise.

Till our aim is won,
Till our work is done,
The stately Mansion built ;
May Blessings descend
On it, and defend
Its hearth from Shame and Guilt.

THE POOR MAN'S DREAM.

I DREAMT I wander'd by the side
Of smiling Delaware ; *
And to my heart with fervour clasp'd
A Maiden, young and fair.
We both had left an English home,
And cross'd the foamy sea,
To seek a dwelling in the West,
The country of the Free !

* A river in the United States.

And *there* I won with ceaseless toil
    The fields and lands around ;
My flocks increas'd and brought me wealth,
    And God my harvests crown'd.
But, ah ! there oft would silent come
    A wish to view the shore,
The dear old Land, which never we
    Might hope to see once more.

We wept together for the Past,
    In God we placed our trust,
And prayed that He would kindly guide
    Our lives with mercy just.
Then when the snows of Winter fell,
    We piled with logs the fire,
And spoke of those we left behind
    As though we ne'er should tire.

Our children clapp'd their tiny hands,
    And laughed with childish glee ;
Or fondly gazing in my face,
    Would nestle on my knee.
While on each quiet Sabbath day,
    They sang some simple hymn,
Which we had learnt in other times,
    E'er clouds our life could dim.

And when the rose of Summer came
    With sunshine, birds, and flowers;
We pluck'd the fruit, and reap'd the corn,
    And proudly called them *ours*.
We thought no more of mills and looms,
    Or England's sadd'ning theme
Of pain and want, of toil and rags,
    But, lo! it was *a dream!*

THE CHILDREN OF THE PLOUGH.

Oh! England hath her noble Sons,
    Who for their Mother land
Will dangers brave, and ever toil
    For Her with heart and hand.
For her the Seaman guides his bark
    O'er Ocean's frowning waves;
For her the Miner calm explores
    Earth's dark and gloomy caves;
For her the Engine pants and roars;
    The Weaver's shuttles fly;
And from the bright and ruddy Forge
    The sparks ascend on high.

Ah! well may England dare be proud
    Of all her treasures now,
And clasp her Darlings to her heart—
    The Children of the Plough.

God bless the Children of the Plough,
    For their's a noble aim ;
The fruits of Peace, of Love, and Joy
    Alone they fain would claim ;
Nor seek the crimson wreath of War,
    Around their brows to twine,
Nor darken with the Cannon's smoke
    The ever glad sunshine.
They war but with the stubborn Soil,
    The Frost, the Wind, and Rain,
And "Hurrah for the Harvest Home,"
    Is Labour's triumph strain ;
They seek no laurels from the fields
    Where thousands dying bow ;
Nor pale-faced weeping Mourners curse
    The Children of the Plough.

Then Hurrah! for the Spade and the Hoe,
    The tillers of the Plain ;
And Hurrah ! for the smiling fields
    Of rich and waving Grain.

And Hurrah! for the giant Steam,
　　Who aids the Farmers' hands,
And gives him strength to triumph o'er
　　The once uncultur'd lands.
Long may the ample Harvests fill
　　And crown the garner's store,
To bring enjoyment to the Rich,
　　And comfort to the Poor.
And long may kindred mortals meet
　　Around the board as now, *
To swell the cheer which hails the toast—
　　"The Children of the Plough."

PULL THROUGH.

Though Dangers rise your path to bar,
　　　　Pull Through, pull through;
Though dimly shines your guiding Star,
　　　　Pull Through, pull through;
For those who now your worth despise,
Who clog your way with Scorn and Lies,
Will haste to Crown you as you rise;
　　　　Pull Through, pull through.

* Written on the occasion of an Agricultural Meeting.

Your deeds let no Dishonour taint,
      Pull Through, pull through ;
Though Worn and Weary never faint,
      Pull Through, pull through ;
Gird on your armour for the Fight,
And nobly battle for the Right,
Heedless of the frowns of Might,
      Pull Through, pull through.

Though Bright Eyes seldom on you gleam,
      Pull Through, pull through ;
Though Vict'ry seem an empty dream,
      Pull Through, pull through ;
For if the Laurel you would wear,
Your heart must learn to Do and Dare,
The Martyr's cross awhile to bear ;
      Pull Through, pull through.

JOHN POUNDS, THE FOUNDER OF RAGGED SCHOOLS.

John Pounds was born at Portsmouth in 1766. In early life he
became a cripple, and betook himself to the "gentle craft." In
a lowly abode in St. Mary-street, he followed his calling, and
originated the present system of industrial schools. The noble-
hearted fellow allowed the little children who played in the
streets to come into his workroom, and learn reading, writing,
and arithmetic of him. He never received, nor would receive,
any recompense for his trouble; and his chief reward was in
beholding those whom he had taught in childhood prove good
and honest in their manhood. He died January 1st, 1839.
Poor as he was, no man ever exceeded him in real usefulness,
and if merit had its true reward in this world, no man could
have claimed a loftier position than John Pounds, the humble
Shoemaker of Portsmouth.

A PRIZE awaits the courtly Bard,
    Whose voice exultant rings
With high laudations of the deeds
    Of crown'd and ermin'd Kings.
The High and Favour'd of the land
    Will smiles on him bestow,
While off'rings rich and presents rare
    From Rank and Wealth will flow.

But what of him who sings the Wrongs,
　The Sorrow and Despair,
Of those who toil till life but seems
　A weary round of Care?
No princely hands will wreath his brow
　With Laurels as of old;
No golden chain, nor jewels rare
　His form may dare enfold!

But what of that? the PEOPLE claim
　The Bard for them alone;
From *Them* will he select his theme,
　And Their applauses own.
What nobler subject for his pen
　Than Him who on his seat
Pursued his toil, yet taught and sav'd
　The Children from the Street?

Far nobler he than King or Peer—
　As on his bench he sat,
Surrounded by his little School,
　His Birds, and Dog, and Cat.
True, he was poor! Was Homer rich,
　Or cynic Socrates?
Does Wealth alone make mortals great,
　Or other Fate's decrees?

No! no—the poor Shoemaker there
    No rich reward might claim;
No tomb of marble pure and white
    Records his honour'd name;
Yet in his Heart he felt a bliss,
    To mortals seldom known,
And held within his breast a Joy
    That others might not own.

Oh! brave John Pounds! oh! noble Heart,
    Whose deeds of goodness shame
The paltry schemes of Statesmen proud
    Who talk themselves to Fame!
He solv'd the Problem of the Age—
    And taught neglected Youth,
To leave the ways of vice and sin
    For those of God and Truth!

A WORKMAN'S WOOING.

I KNOW that my hands may be hard and rough,
    That my cheek may be worn and pale;
But my heart is made of a good sound stuff
    That never will falter or fail;

C

And though in the World with my mates I stand
   To share in the Battle of Life,
I take thee, my Girl, by thy dainty hand,
   As my own, my bonny sweet Wife.

Though never a jewelled wreath may span
   The curls on thy beautiful brow,
I'll pledge thee my Heart and Truth as a Man,
   And love thee for ever as now ;
And though the bright dreams of Love's sunny prime
   Too often the Future belie,
The steep hills of Life together we'll climb,
   And conquer our fate—Thou and I.

My coat may be poor, my words be but few,
   Yet there's never an ermin'd King
Can offer his Queen a present more true
   Than mine of a Heart and a Ring ;
That tiny gold link, with which we may bind
   Our fortunes in one common bond ;
And rear us a home where Happiness shrin'd
   May dwell with Affection most fond.

What more would we seek ?   What more would we
     have ?
   What more could fair Nature bestow ?
If, of all her gifts, we ventur'd to crave
   The richest that mortals might know.

For aye, dearest Girl, shall our wedded love
    Flash—Star-like—a-top of our life ;
And never will I a base traitor prove
    To my Heart, my Home, or my Wife !

THE CANKER IN THE ROSE.

THEY say our land's a favour'd clime,
    Where slaves can never be—
Where Truth may boldly stand erect,
    And Thought may flourish free.
We boast the wonders of the Loom,
    The Engine, and the Mine ;
We count the sails which bear our name
    To lands beyond the brine ;
Yet 'neath the glitter and the glare,
    A stream of sorrow flows ;
Which *may*, perchance, o'erwhelm our land—
    A Canker in the Rose !

Go ! view the poor man's squalid lane ;
    His hovel, bleak and small ;
Where pallid spectres starve and slave,
    With scarce the strength to crawl ;

And leave their children in the streets,
   The bread of crime to win ;
To ripen for the hangman's touch,
   And be our shame and sin.
What are the glories of our State ?—
   If none may interpose
To stay this dark and deadly blight—
   This Canker in the Rose !

We raise the Cross—the Gospel preach
   To nations wide and far ;
From Zone to Zone, from Pole to Pole,
   There's nought our path can bar.
Our rulers breathe with sentence bland,
   How England dares to cope
With King or Czar, with Serf or Slave,
   With Kaisar, or with Pope ;
And yet too oft they *will* ignore
   The sorrows, wrongs, and woes,
Of those who toil for England's wealth,
   Oh ! Canker in the Rose !

Meanwhile, a distant murmur low,
   The list'ner oft may hear,
A cry that breathes of evil days,
   Of tempests drawing near.

The starving forms, so lately scorned,
   May in their hatred turn
On those who dared their lot despise,
   And their appeal could spurn.
Oh ! may our statesmen be forewarn'd
   To check this ill which grows
In silence dark, with giant strength,
   A Canker in the Rose !

THE LABOURER'S SON.

The incidents on which the following lines are founded, were related to the author during a discussion on the policy of the game laws. The father is supposed to be speaking.

Ah ! John, he was a noble youth—
   And I, methinks, can see him now,
With God's own stamp of earnest truth,
   Imprinted on his manly brow.
But we were poor, so very poor,
   That oft we lacked our daily bread,
Till we our fate could scarce endure,
   But anguish'd wish'd that we were dead.

They bade us work, and work we sought,
    But hands were many ; wages scant ;
And though we onward hopeful fought,
    We could not keep ourselves from want.

The Winter came with cold keen blast,
    With ruthless frost, and blinding snow :
And men were forced to cease at last
    From toil, and idly homewards go.
We had no food, nor fire to warm
    Our wasted frames and trembling hands ;
While round our cottage howl'd the storm
    O'er frozen streams, and snow-wrapt lands.
My boy went forth, I knew not where,
    From me a weary day he staid ;
Then he return'd and brought a hare,
    From whence obtained he never said.

But two rough keepers, rushing in,
    Their prisoner—my son—did claim :
My heart leapt wild my breast within,
    And down I knelt in grief and shame.
Before the Justice soon he stood,
    His moisten'd eyes fix'd on the ground,
While I for mercy for him sued,
    And for him offer'd to be bound.

But " poachers had increased of late,
   No mercy really could be shown,—
Three months in gaol must be his fate : "
   Thus Justice spake, with icy tone.

Those three months pass'd, I know not how,
   And then my boy I saw again ;
Oh, God ! how changed was his brow,
   With his imprisonment and pain.
" Where is my Mother ? "—" Son, she's dead."
   " And where is Lucy ? "—" She is gone."
" All gone," he shriek'd, and bow'd his head,
   And stood as if transfix'd to stone.
Henceforth he was an alter'd man,
   And wander'd in the world apart ;
Intent on some deep, secret plan,
   Which silent grew within his heart.

At length he bade to me farewell,
   To Canada he meant to go :
I felt my breast with anguish swell,
   And sank beneath the cruel blow.
'Twas for our good, he now has won,
   With the rough labour of his hands,
A home which he can call his own,
   Surrounded with his smiling lands.

And he has bade me to him come,
    His happiness and joy to share :
Soon shall I leave my English home,
    To dwell in comfort with him there.

Oh ! England, if thou wouldst retain
    Thy strength and power e'en as of yore,
Let not thy children plead in vain,
    Nor thoughtless crush the helpless poor :
But rather with a kindly hand,
    The outcast seek, the fallen raise ;
From them no more in coldness stand,
    But train their young to better ways :
Else, oh ! beware, there is a God—
    All nations reap as they have sown ;
Beware ! lest thou in wrath be trod,
    And peace to thee no more be known.

THE EMIGRANT'S SONG.

WESTWARD, Ho ! for the Delaware !
Westward, Ho ! for the Sckuylkil's wave :
A Freeman's home awaits us there—
There, where Toil its reward may have.

To thee—Old Land—we bid farewell,
Thou wert to us a hopeless land :
Yet with a sigh we break the spell
Which binds us to thy foam-wash'd strand.
Westward, Ho ! where the fields are green ;
Westward, Ho ! where the corn waves high ;
And rich fruits smile the boughs between,
Flush'd and warm 'neath the cloudless sky.
Westward, Ho! for the Delaware !
Westward, Ho! for the Sckuylkil's wave ;
A Freeman's home awaits us there :
Land of the Free, the Good, and Brave.

Then, Westward, Ho! Boys! Westward, Ho!
With hopeful hearts we cross the main,
Our souls with Freedom's flame aglow,
No longer link'd to Care or Pain.
Far, far, from Tyrant's that oppress,
Who soul and body long have ground,
And wrung their wealth from pale distress,
Nor to their madness placed a bound.
Westward, Ho ! with our brawny hands,
Westward, Ho! with our limbs so strong,
To win, with toil, the teeming lands,
And sing the Freeman's·proudest song.
Westward, Ho ! for the Delaware !
Westward, Ho ! for the Sckuylkil's wave ;
A Freeman's home awaits us there :
Land of the Free, the Good, and Brave.

HARD TIMES.*

FROM o'er the broad Atlantic wave,
    A note of terror comes ;
Which brings despair to English hearts,
    And dearth to English homes.
Our Mills are clos'd, our Looms are still,
    Our Engines silent rust ;
Our massive Bales of wares are left
    To moulder in the dust :
While pallid Forms, with aching hands,
    Press close their fever'd brow,
For evil days are drawing near—
    God help the Workman now !

With Foodless shelves, and Fireless grates,
    We scarce know whence to turn :
There is no Work : we must forego
    The Bread we fain would earn.
With gloomy thoughts our souls are rife,
    Dark scowls each anxious eye :
We *cannot* see our Children pale,
    In silence starve and die!

* Written during the Commercial Panic of 1857-58.

Though—far more blest than *we*—they leave
 A world where we must bow,
For evil days are drawing near—
 God help the Workman now !

Our statesmen war with rival creeds,
 Intent on Party aim,
And leave us in our bitter needs,
 The Pauper's alms to claim.
The hands which toil'd with honest zeal,
 In Fact'ry, or in Mine,
Are left to starve, while Lords may sport,
 And sip their Clubhouse wine ;
Still iron Mammon bids us toil
 As heretofore—But how ?
For evil days are drawing near—
 God help the Workman now !

Oh ! ye who roll in luxury,
 Ye Lords of Gold and Land,
Of your excess a portion spare,
 To feed the famish'd band.
The Earth is God's. Its fulness fair
 For *all* was sure ordain'd,
Beware ! lest ye a sin commit,
 And die with conscience stain'd :

Men! rather take the better path,
   And Want with help endow ;
For God will bless the kindly hearts
   That aid the workman now !

TIMES OF WANT.

Oh ! Mary they have closed the Mill,
   The looms are silent now ;
And we must stoop with heavy souls
   Beneath the rod to bow.
I feel a throbbing in my heart—
   A chill within my breast—
And long to lay my weary form
   Within the grave to rest ;
For life has been a ceaseless strife
   With cares that ever grew ;
We slav'd, and starv'd, and NOW, alas !
   Oh ! God ! what shall we do ?

I've seen thee weep, when thou did'st think
   Thy tears I could not see ;
And seen thee put aside thy food
   That baby fed might be ;

While oft thou forced a loving smile,
  Although thy heart was sore ;
And kiss'd my pale and bloodless cheek,
  And bade me grieve no more.
But now thou cans't not hide thy tears ;
  Thy lips they quiver, too ;
Thy hand, it trembles in my own ;
  Oh ! God ! what shall we do ?

Thy fingers they are thin and worn
  With needlework so cheap ;
Thy eyes are red, thy brow is cold,
  For want of rest and sleep.
Our little infant, fever'd, droops,
  And soon will be no more :
It had not starv'd had I been rich,
  But I, alas, am poor.
I wonder if the wealthy great
  Would help us if they knew
Our wretched fate ?   The thought is vain ;
  Oh ! God ! what shall we do ?

For never shall these lips of mine,
  A pauper's pittance crave
While I have life, tho' after death
  I fill a pauper's grave.

My soul grows fierce.   Oh ! that my voice
   Could ring throughout the land,
And breathe the cares, the wants, and fate.
   Of Labour's starving band ;
And bid the Lords of Gold beware,
   Lest they, like us, may sue,
When Revolution comes, and cry—
   " Oh ! God ! what shall we do ? "

THE POET'S POWER.

ALONG the weary, gloomy path,
   Which our forefather's trod,
With aching feet, and sadden'd hearts,
   All hopelessly we plod.
Grim Want and Care our steps pursue,
For work is scant, and friends are few.

We view the great ones of the land
   Pass by in lordly state ;
And in our souls we feel arise
   A stern and bitter hate,
That they are RICH, while we are POOR !
That we have LESS, while they have MORE !

But we are human—we have souls,
   A life our life within ;
And moments rise, when we would spurn
   From us the tempter, Sin :
'Tis then we feel the Poet's power,
To cheer and soothe each lonely hour.

'Tis then we bless the pens that strive
   To raise each lowly heart ;
And with their sweet impassion'd strains
   The words of hope impart
To us, poor children of the soil,
Whose few frail years are pass'd in toil.

We bless them that they kindly bade
   Our nobler feelings rise ;
And woke—with touch of genius rare—
   Our inmost sympathies :
For this we love each Poet's name,
And crown them with a household fame.

Oh ! may our aspirations prove
   The triumph of their art,
And bid the joys of Love and Peace
   No more as dreamings start,
Until we feel unto us given
The means to make the Earth a Heaven.

THE DYING WORKMAN.

I AM dying—so they tell me—may be 'tis for the
    best
That these poor aching limbs of mine should have
    some little rest ;
For I've labour'd hard and long, till my cheek was
    pale with care ;
Till my brow was deeply furrow'd, and silver'd was
    my hair.
My feeble strength is ebbing fast, my sight is
    growing dim,
I know that Death is coming now, but have no fear
    of *him*.
Come, kiss me, Wife ; and you, old Ralph, give me
    your horny hand,
In death, aye faithful as in life, by your old mate
    you stand.

These five-and-thirty years, my Man, we've rough'd
    it side by side,
And in our weakness and our strength, we each on
    each relied ;

And now, like to a shatter'd loom, Life's web I
    weave no more ;
But leave this earth of scorn and hate, for Heaven's
    radiant shore.
I hear the strain of golden harps, the sound of angel
    wings,
And feel—*too late!*—I might have dar'd and done
    far nobler things
Than idle all my youth away, Life's mellow sunny
    prime,
Before the frosts of Age had crown'd my head with
    silv'ry rime.

But what was I ?   What was I taught ?   Son of a
    drunken sire ;
Child of a hag, whose fingers plied my lips with
    liquid fire !
Rear'd in the kennel and the street, the filthy slum
    my school,
Where shame-fac'd Vice at Virtue laugh'd, and
    call'd her "slave" and " fool."
Man ! never once my infant lips were taught a word
    of pray'r ;
A wretched English Arab I—I could but lie and swear !
What could I be but what I was?—a sign of
    England's shame !
Place in my stead your noblest man, and *he* would
    be the same.

D

But I was sav'd, as well you know, by that fond
    angel there,
Who, in the guise of wedded Wife, hath made my
    life more fair ;
A tender spell around my heart with winning grace
    she wove,
And sooth'd my rugged nature down with gentle
    words of love.
For *her* I dash'd aside the glass, and brav'd the
    scoff and ban
Of former mates, and stood erect—no more a slave,
    but—MAN !
Methinks the Rulers of the State, too oft but seldom
    know
The debt of gratitude which they to England's
    daughters owe.

Come, Daughter, come ; and you, my Boy ; kneel
    down by me and pray
To Him, the Father of us all, that each may never
    stray
From word of Truth, or path of Right ; but ever
    strive to be
A comfort and a hope to *her* who made life sweet
    to me.

Another kiss, and then good bye; the room is
    growing dark—

I see the gates of gold and pearl—hark! to the
    music, hark!

Good bye—good bye—no more for me will sound
    the fact'ry bell,

The warp of life at last is cut; God bless you all—
    Farewell!

SCAB! SCAB!! SCAB!!!

Or, THE COMBINATIONISTS' LOGIC.

"Scab," "Black Sheep," &c., are terms applied to those work-
men who act against the rules laid down by the generality of
Trades' Unions. This and the two following Songs were
written during the Shoemakers' Strike, at Northampton, in
1858; but it is only fair to state that several Trades' Unions,
such as the Bookbinders', of London, and the Manchester Order
of Smiths', most earnestly deprecate any such conduct on the
part of their members.

Hunt him here, and hunt him there,
Shop-mates, hunt him ev'rywhere;
Let each sot and drunken drab,
Join the chase, and hunt the "scab."

What's his crime ?   He works for bread,
For little Charley—sick in bed.
Nothing else ?   His wife is poor ;
He fain would make his income more.
Is that all ?   He will not join
Our ranks, and with us all combine.
He dares to think ; and dares be free ;
Things which never more must be ;
For liberty is all a flam :
The People's progress all a sham :
And Bomba is our model king,
So we with glee will ever sing—

      Hunt him here, and hunt him there,
      Shop-mates, hunt him ev'rywhere ;
      Let each sot and drunken drab,
      Join the chase, and hunt the "scab."

What of our hearts ?   Oh ! they are stone,
Nor love nor mercy e'er will own.
Our interests ?   Oh ! fudge and stuff ;
We pay ourselves, and that's enough.
For our pleasure and our play
We have our shillings four a day.*
But are you just ?   Don't know or care :
Ask me no more, or I will swear !

* An allusion to the payment received by the "Strike" officials.

For law, for justice, or for right,
We do not care a blessed mite!
Not common sense shall be our plan;
We'll rule by force, by fear, and ban;
And woe to him who dares to see
Things in another light than we;
For every thing we say is law:
Now there's my speech, I'll say no more.

Hunt him here, and hunt him there,
Shopmates, hunt him ev'rywhere;
Let each sot and drunken drab,
Join the chase, and hunt the "scab."

But why do you to him deny
His right the case himself to try?
Because we cannot make him see,
That he ought never to be free
To choose his trade, or do his best
To serve and aid his interest.
Oh! nonsense! what is that to you?
There's work enough for all to do.
Ah! yes; but then we want to keep
It to ourselves, that none may reap
The slightest share; but starve and slave
In workhouse yards, or find a grave.
Nay, this is wrong! Well, wrong or right,
For this I'll clench my fist and fight;

No scholar I, but this I know,
The weakest to the wall shall go,

Hunt him here, and hunt him there,
Shopmates, hunt him ev'rywhere
Let each sot and drunken drab,
Join the chase, and hunt the "scab."

THE TYRANTS OF THE LAST.

Shame, shame, on ye all, False sons of the Last :
Base traitors to Freedom and Right !
Who o'er us, poor toilers, seek but to cast
The chains of your folly and might.
What do you care, that a poor man may sigh
In vain for a morsel of bread?
No work let him have : no ! let the fool die,
And rot like a dog when he's dead ;
Aye, let his poor widow in wretchedness pine,
Or perish in bitter despair ;
Let Hunger and Sorrow relentlessly twine
Their claws on his children so fair !

Shame on ye, Dastards ; go, hasten abroad
   Where kings in their tyranny reign :
Down, down, on your knees, hail each for your lord,
   And worship the Scaffold and Chain.
For what are ye all, but mimics of those—
   Who Justice and Liberty ban,
And set themselves up as the bloodiest foes
   Of Freedom, of Truth, and of Man ?
Hounding our daughters, like wolves, thro' the town,
   Reviling our sisters and wives,
Hooting and yelling our poor children down,
   And bidding them flee for their lives.

Shame on ye, Cowards ! Oh ! can ye be men
   With reason, with sense, or with thought,
To act like the brute, which growls in its den,
   And glares in its fury when caught.
Go ! hire yourselves to the Pope, or the Czar,
   And no longer in England remain :
Here on our daughters ye shall not make war,
   Or your power for mischief retain.
This is no country for tyrants or slaves,—
   This land of the brave and the free ;
Curs, hie ye away beyond the salt waves,
   With Louis and Pius to be.

ON STRIKE.

Oh ! my Brothers ! pause and listen,
   Ere the Sorrow and the Tears
Cause each sunken Eye to glisten
   With the Grief of after-years ;
Ere the wretched Mothers, weeping,
   Sob as though their hearts would break,
For their infant Darlings sleeping,
   And their thoughtless Husbands' sake ;
Ere ye tramp on lonely Highways,
   Through the Village or the Town,
Or in Cities' crowded by-ways,
   Sadly wander up and down ;
For employment ever seeking
   Where there's none, alas ! to give,
Till the Hunger-glance is speaking
   That ye scarce know how to live.

True, our path is often dreary—
   True, the Joy-hopes seldom shine,
Cheering hearts with labour weary,
   In the Fact'ry, Field, or Mine ;—
True, that Sin and Shame oppress us,
   In each Court, and Lane, and Street,

Where but Angels few may bless us
　　With their smiles so pure and sweet;
True it is, our Children dying
　　From the poison breath of Drain,
Oft with fevered lips are sighing
　　For their daily Bread in vain.
Whilst we Toilers, bowed with anguish,
　　Aged grow before our day;
And in Pauper hovels languish
　　Till our Spirits glide away.

But these Ills last not for ever,
　　Not all Iron is our chain,
Not all hopeless each Endeavour
　　To remove the olden stain
Round our Hearts for ever clinging,
　　Filling them with Scorn and Hate,
Truth and Reason from them flinging,
　　Till we murmur at our Fate,—
Murmur at the Rich man's treasures,
　　At his Houses, at his Wine,
At his dearly purchas'd Pleasures,
　　At his Halls which lighted shine;—
But, my Brothers, murmurs never
　　Taught our Souls the crown to win;
Or with lofty Courage sever
　　Every link of Vice and Sin.

Not by "Striking," or by spurning
  Ev'ry boon which Science brings,—
With the aid of Art and Learning,
  Shall we rise to nobler things.
Honest toil, and Temp'rate living,
  Manly educated mind ;
Earnest soul, and Heart forgiving,
  Are the means in each enshrin'd ;
With their aid, each ill degrading
  We may swift from us remove,
And around us weave unfading
  Wreaths of Joy, of Peace, and Love.
Now, my Brothers, I have ended,
  And my simple Strain is o'er ;
If ye deem truth with it blended,
  Go ye forth and "Strike" no more.

THE COUNTRY AND THE TOWN.

THUS spoke the Country to the Town :—
  Oh! Sister, are they true,
These evil things which people speak,
  And dare ascribe to you ?

I hear of loathsome courts and lanes,
   Where Vice and Fever dwell ;
Where Crime and Hate, and Shame and Sin
   Combine for purpose fell :

Where selfish parents drain the glass,
   Nor Love, nor Pity feel,
But bid their offspring roam the streets,
   To starve, or lie, or steal !
Where brutal fiends break the vows
   At God's high altar made :
And kill the partners of their life
   By blows, or crimson'd blade ;

Where painted harlots frenzied smile,
   Or laugh in wild despair ;
Or reckless leap the silent Bridge,
   And end their anguish *there !*
Oh ! Sister—Dearest Sister—hear
   The fond appeal from me—
Arise, and in thy strength sublime,
   Say these no more shall be.

Then to the Country spake the Town :—
   Why dost thou cast the stone ?
Art *thou* less stain'd with crime than I ?
   Canst thou less evil own ?

I have no ricks for Hate to burn ;
  Nor woods where keepers' hide,
To mark the poachers' crouching form
  Through fern and grasses glide.

Hast thou less offspring born of shame,
  Our lasting stain to be ?
From drunken brawls and brutal fights,
  Say, Sister, art thou free ?
Then said the Country to the town—
  We *both* are in the wrong,
We *both* have err'd, we *both* have fell,
  And yet we both are strong.

Then let us both with cheerful Zeal,
  With Gentleness and Love,
With Mercy, Hope, and Faith divine,
  These evils dare remove.
Nor each reproach with gibe and scorn,
  Nor mutual strife endure ;
But raise our children from the dust,
  And bid them sin no more.

JOHN O'NEILL.

One of the most promising signs of the time, is the persistent
efforts made by a large section of the toiling masses, to elevate
themselves from the social and political degradation which the
misfortune of centuries has imposed upon them. In the pro-
motion of their noble endeavours, they have no lack of leaders,
or writers, such as John O'Neill, whose pen gave utterance to
many a poem, full of intense fervour, on behalf of his fellow-
toilers; and of stern unflinching denunciation of their merciless
enemy and everlasting bane—INTEMPERANCE. He died,
almost unknown, save by name, a few months since, in London.

In times of old the Grecian bards
    Deem'd Bacchus god divine ;
And with a lively measure sang
    In praise of rosy Wine :
They hail'd it as the source of bliss —
    The nectar sweet of Jove ;—
The true and loving friend of Man,
    Of Harmony, and Love.
With Ivy garlands would they crown
    The Idol of their song ;
And with the tabor, fife, and drum
    They join'd the Satyr throng.

" But *they* were heathens," some will say,
     " And *we* are Christians now ;
We own no mythic Ruler's sway,
     Nor to such idols bow ! "
Men, is this true ?   Hath never Bard
     Sang in these later days
Of Wine—of *Wine*—of rosy WINE !
     In notes of joy and praise ?
Had Burns no voice, Mackay, nor Moore,
     The soul to stir and move,
To send the passions mounting high,
     And Life's destruction prove ?

While Gin-mad slaves in frenzy clasp
     The soul consuming chain,
And let their famish'd offspring pine
     In hunger, cold, and pain ;
Or roam the wet and stony streets,
     To earn the bread of crime ;
And on the frowning Gallows mock
     Our Bible-creed sublime !
While gilded temples ope their doors—
     Where lights and mirrors glare—
Where meet the Harlot and the Thief
     To drown remorse and care.

Is this the Poet's mission true ?
  The lesson he should preach ?
To praise the gay handmaid of crime,
  And her enticements teach !
No, no ! the high and noble aim
  To each great Singer given,
Is e'er to lead men's erring hearts
  From things of Earth to Heaven :
To elevate each mortal mind ;
  To bid us *think* and *feel ;*
To do our best for fellow kind,
  As did poor John O'Neill.

THE OLD, OLD TALE.

Oh ! how I flutter'd in his arms—
  His heart's own darling dove—
And gaz'd upon his manly brow,
  All flush'd with hope and love.
He told me that his hands were strong,
  The world was free and wide :
Would I forsake my childhood's home
  And be his bonny bride ?

Five happy years in joyance sped—
    Five happy years of bliss—
Since I, with fond assenting smile,
    First crown'd his happiness.
Three prattling children bless'd our love,
    And climb'd their father's knee
To seek his bright and tender gaze ;
    Oh ! who more glad than we ?

Another year.   How chang'd the scene !
    A happy home no more !
A weeping wife, and offspring pale,
    In silence watch the door ;
Till stagg'ring footsteps on the stairs
    Bid them all startled flee
Their drunken father's sad return
    From madden'd revelry.

" Come, woman, brandy give me quick ! "
    With fury wild he cried.
" No ! husband, *never !* by my soul, "
    In sternness I replied.
I mark'd the fearful demon look—
    The clench'd determin'd hand—
Extended arm—low mutter'd curse—
    And scarce with fear could stand.

Blow after blow upon me fell ;
   Our little children cried :
Another blow ; and oh, my God !
   The aim from me was *wide*.
I heard a low and stifl'd wail,—
   Oh ! how my heart did thrill ;
A darkness seem'd to cloud my sight—
   A sob—and all was still.

The morning light in brightness shone
   Upon the chamber floor,   .
Where lay my child, with bleeding brow,
   To rise in life no more.
His little curls, so soft and fair,
   With blood were damp and cold ;
No more my arms his tender form
   In fond embrace might hold.

Alas ! that fatal, bitter morn,
   How could I calm my woe ?
My sober'd husband's breaking heart
   The truth could scarcely know.
In yon churchyard my darling lies ;
   And o'er the blue salt sea,
His father pines—exil'd from home,
   From Hope, and Love, and Me.

GLIMPSES OF THE FUTURE.

Ever yearning, as of Old, in these days of Steam
and Gold,
  For the Glorious, the Beautiful, the Happy, and
  the Free,
A thousand gentle fancies in the Dreamer's breast
unfold,
In all their purple ripeness, with their visions
uncontroll'd,
  Of the bright and sinless Future which our fallen
  world shall see.

When no more shall Toilers sigh, nor their palefac'd
Children cry—
  In their squalid hovels crouching in each fever
  reeking room—
For one moment with the Flowers, 'neath the
pleasant country sky,
With the grass below their feet, with the branches
waving high,
  Till forgotten are their Sorrows, all their Misery,
  and Doom.

When the crimson cloud of War never more shall
    dim the star
  Of our Happiness and household Joys, or cast
    its fatal shade
O'er the troubl'd path of Man, and his aspirations
    mar,
Till—a prodigal of Hate—from the Right he
    wanders far,
  And the golden fruit of Love and Hope before
    him lie decay'd.

When no more shall Passion blind, nor dark
    Ignorance shall bind
  With the selfwrought chain of Vice and Shame—
    the links and gyves of Sin—
God's own noblest gift to Man, in our mortal frame
    enshrin'd,
Fair Creation's masterpiece—The illimitable MIND,
  Which, enfranchis'd from its thrall, shall a crown
    of triumph win.

When poor Labour's weary heart never more shall
    fiercely start
  With the reckless jealousy of Class—the hatred
    deep and stern—

Such as only those can feel who have borne the
    bitter smart
Of viewing all their nearest and their dearest ones
    depart,
    For the lack of warmth and food which they
    would, but *could* not, earn.

When the Sun of Truth shall shine with a radiance
    divine,
    Evermore suffusing with a joy each bud which
    decks the sod ;
While Content around each soul shall, like clinging
    ivy, twine,
Till the nations of the Earth in one brotherhood
    combine,
    Each united in one common creed, and to one
    father—GOD !

NORTHAMPTONSHIRE

RAMBLES, INCIDENTS,

AND

LEGENDS.

NORTHAMPTONSHIRE RAMBLES,

&c., &c.

THE CHARNEL VAULT AT ROTHWELL.

Several years ago a vault was discovered beneath the ancient
Church at Rothwell, or "Rowell," in which was contained an
immense number of human skulls and bones, regularly piled in
layers, and said to consist entirely of remains belonging to men
of large stature. The origin of this extraordinary collection
has never been satisfactorily ascertained, although many writers
of learning and eminence have attempted to solve the enigma.
The local tradition attributes the remains to be those of the
slain in a great conflict, supposed to have taken place near to,
or at, Rothwell, in ancient times, when the place was—according
to some writers—the metropolis of that part of England.
A charter fair is held here every year, on which occasion the
vault is open for public inspection.

Down to the vault— the gloomy Vault—with cau-
    tious steps we go ;
Down to the charnel-house of Death, the olden
    porch below.

The air around feels cold and damp, the taper
waxeth dim,

While fancy fills the sombre shades with grisly
phantoms grim.

WITHOUT—a laughing crowd surrounds the show-
man's grinning mimes ;

Within—a pile of fleshless bones tells us of other
times.

WITHOUT—the day is passing fair—the sunlight
gems the flowers ;

Within—'midst darkness, skulls, and bones, we,
sadden'd, muse for hours.

Strange problem of the mystic Past—shall Man the
curtain lift ?

Or, shall the swelling sands of Time still o'er the
secret drift ?

That we may never know to whom these whiten'd
bones belong'd ;

Or on what field of peace or strife, in love or hate
they throng'd.

Swell'd they the Norman's robber ranks ?   Came
they in prow of Dane ?

Or rais'd they high the Saxon's flag across the
Northern main ?

Or were they sons of mighty Rome, whose stern and
fearless tramp

Oft scar'd the wolves that ventur'd near the earth-
work bounded camp ?

Perchance they were of Harold's race, and when he
    wounded fell,
On Hastings' plain, the tidings flew o'er valley,
    hill, and dell,
Till Rothwell's wall-girt town it reached, and cries
    for vengeance rang
High o'er the clash of shields and swords, o'er
    spears and bucklers clang !
But why recount the tale of blood ? The Saxons
    fought in vain ;
And blue-ey'd maids, and matrons pale, wept o'er
    the murder'd slain ;
While aged monks, with trembling hands, piled up
    the ghastly dead,
For whom no requiem was sung, nor priestly prayer
    was said.

But who can tell, or who can part, the Mythic from
    the Real ;
And from these eyeless, fleshless, skulls the rays of
    Knowledge steal ?
In Learning, Science, Art, and Skill, men daily
    grow more wise ;
Yet still the portals of the Past each Vandal hand
    defies.
Like us, men liv'd, and lov'd, and sung--for baubles
    fought and died ;
And bow'd them down to earthly gods, in ignorance
    and pride.

Yet why should we regret their fate? They had no
   hopes above
The Northern Gods, whose spell hath wan'd before
   the Cross of Love.

THE MONUMENTS IN WARKTON CHURCH.

In St. Edmund's Church, Warkton, are four very sumptuous
   monuments to the Montagu family. That of John, Duke of
   Montagu, ob. 1794, and Mary, Duchess of Montagu, ob. 1751,
   are by Roubilliac; and that of Mary, Duchess of Buccleuch,
   ob. 1775, is by Peter Matthias Van Gelder; the fourth was
   erected a few years since, to the memory of Elizabeth Montagu, Duchess Dowager of Buccleuch. The cenotaphs are
   placed in a part of the church built expressly for their reception, and in their union of beauty, taste, sentiment, and work-
   manship, they are probably unsurpassed by any of the same
   class in Europe. Had they been placed in a cathedral, they
   would have attracted the attention of thousands, and have
   escaped from an obscurity which they do not deserve.

I BARE my brow and stand alone
   To muse in silence on the Art,
Which from the cold and senseless stone
   Can bid the Dreams of Fancy start;

And with the hand of skill renew
   The features of the dead and gone,
Till—as the moveless forms we view—
   We stay each tear and cease to mourn.
No marvel that the wealthy Great
   Their marble cenotaphs should rear,
Where studied groups, in changeless state,
   And grave and classic guise appear.
Yet, oft I think a humble grave
   In some quaint churchyard, green and old,
Where stately trees their branches wave,
   And cast their shadows o'er the wold,
I should prefer : for *There* might fall
   The tear of pure Affection sweet,
Too oft restrain'd in princely hall,
   Where Rank, and Wealth, and Beauty meet.
A simple headstone, with my name,
   A few wild flow'rets from the woods,
Are all that I in death would claim,
   In these calm rustic solitudes.
'Tis true no eyes might gaze in awe
   On sculptur'd urn, or tablet proud ;
No stately monument procure
   The wonder of the heedless Crowd.
But then the birds would ever sing
   High o'er my tomb ; and violets blue
Their rich and fragrant incense fling
   Where cowslips pale primroses woo ;

And village Maids perchance might wend
    Their way, my resting place beside,
To meet some Swain or loving Friend
    In whom their hearts might dare confide.
And here sometimes the Old might come,
    Their weary aching limbs to rest ;
And dream of that bright promis'd home
    Where smile the Angel Singers blest ;
Or when the Children flock around,
    And bid them some old tale relate,
Might point unto the grassy mound,
    And tell them of the Poet's fate :
How oft his humble pen had sought
    To cheer each fellow toiler's heart,
With gems from secret mines of thought,
    Or songs which could a joy impart ;
Of how he battled for the Right,
    And spurn'd the sophistries of Wrong ;
And learnt in suff"ring all his might,
    And found his Weakness made him Strong !

THE CASTLE CLOSE, BARTON SEAGRAVE.

The Castle, built by Nicholas de Seagrave, Marshal of England, in the time of Edward II., was situated here. Popular tradition asserts that the destruction of the fortress took place, by the orders of Cromwell, during the period of the Civil Wars. The only vestiges now existing are the mound on which the castle was built, and the surrounding trench which formed the moat. The neighbouring church of St. Botolph's bears unmistakable marks of its Saxon origin, and, despite its motley additions, forms an object of interest for the antiquary.

Oh! beautiful Barton, how oft have I stray'd
    Beneath the green boughs of thy tall stately trees;
Or silently rambled o'er each grassy glade,
    Or rested on some mossy knoll at my ease.
How lovely and quiet the groves seem around,
    How softly and sweetly the Ise stream doth flow;
Still near to the base of the old Castle mound,
    It waters the meads, as in times long ago.
Aye, in times long ago, when Rapine and War,
    O'er England's proud cities, with crimson hand
        sped,
And bade hills and vallies to echo afar,
    The cry of the Dying, the wail for the Dead!

Here England's stern Marshal his castle-home rear'd,
  And often would frown from the battlements high,
In scorn and defiance on foes that appear'd,
  His will and his power to spurn and defy.
Here watch'd the grim Warden all coated in mail—
  Above him the banner would flaunt from the
     wall;
And here Seagrave's Lady oft felt her heart quail,
  Lest in the hot skirmish her husband should fall.
Here in the bright sunshine each knightly lance
     gleam'd,
  As proudly, yet gaily, they rode to the fray;
Or fought in the tilt-yard, or lazily dream'd
  Of Beauty's fair smile, or of wars far away.

But where are they now—those fierce Spirits bold,
  Whose shout from the turrets so grandly would
     ring—
Whose swords gleam'd so brightly, as in times of
     old,
  Defending their Castle, their Lord, and their
     King?
The red flames shot high from the grey batter'd
     wall,
  The last brave retainer lay stretch'd in his gore,
Ere Cromwell's stern legions could enter the hall,
  Where Cavaliers gaily should meet never more.

Chang'd, chang'd is the scene, May blossoms now
    bloom,
And fond lovers roam, their sweet secrets to tell ;
The sunshine of Peace long hath banish'd the
    gloom—
The heart-rending sorrows of War's bitter spell.

MARY OF VALENCE.

The Castle of Fotheringhay was once in the possession of Mary
of Valence, or Valentia, who was married to Audemare, Earl of
Pembroke, who fell in a tournament on the day of the nuptials;
whence she is characterised by the poet Gray, as the

> "Sad Chatillion, on her bridal morn,
> That wept her bleeding love."

The castle is not now in existence.

On ! bright was the dawning
Of that Summer morning ;
When the lark carol'd high o'er the dew spangled lea,
And blossoms were springing,
Their rich odours flinging
On the soft balmy wind as it swept by each tree.

The helmets were glancing,
The chargers were prancing,
The silk pennons waved in the warm sunny rays ;
The joy-bells were ringing,
The minstrels were singing
To the music of harps, in brave Audemare's praise.

With heart pleasure-laden,
She call'd to each maiden
To deck her with roses, and with gems bind her hair,
But one simple blossom
To place on her bosom,
And, "Oh ! I am ready; where's my Audemare fair?"

Still smile, Lady Mary ;
Nor mark how they tarry,
The gay champions and knights of thy own Audemare :
For soon will thy gladness
Be chang'd into sadness,
And the joy of thy heart unto sorrow and care.

Hark ! hear the monk singing—
His voice mournful ringing
Through the woodland and glen—a wild dirge for
the dead ;
Or sentences holy,
As sadly and slowly
The arm'd serfs bear the corpse from the field where
it bled.

Still nearer and nearer—
The chant swelling clearer—
The litter approacheth the grey castle walls ;
Woe, woe, to the Maiden !
The tidings—death laden—
Oh ! who shall convey to those old Norman halls ?

But Love has its feelings,
Its mystic revealings,
That e'er warn the fond heart of ills hovering near :
Her brow lost its brightness ;
Her soul lost its lightness ;
And her sunshine of life seem'd all clouded and
drear.

Her smile lost its sweetness,
As with madden'd fleetness
Through the courtyard, 'neath archway, o'er draw-
bridge, she flew
Past warder, past archer,
Past startled road marcher,
Till she reach'd the pale form of her Audemare true.

With deep lamentations—
With fierce exclamations—
Did she kiss the blue lips, in her frenzied despair :
Then sobbing, fell fainting,
Her Lover's blood tainting
Her white bridal roses, and his love-scarf so fair !

F

THE FUNERAL OF MARY, QUEEN OF SCOTS.

After the execution of Mary, Queen of Scots, at Fotheringhay, Elizabeth directed the body of her victim to be interred with royal honours, in the ancient cathedral of Peterborough. Several chroniclers have given an account of the funeral, which reads like a hideous mockery, after the treatment to which Mary had been subjected during her lifetime.

Aye! crown her *now*, poor murder'd Queen,
  Ye titled mourners kneel,
And stimulate the grief and pain
  Your hearts could never feel,
When, in her prison'd wretchedness,
  For liberty she sigh'd ;
Or strove in vain with tears and prayers,
  To melt the Tudor's pride.

Let tapers blaze, and pennons wave,
  And wardens line the hall ;
Let shields display their antique charms
  Above the sombre pall ;
What boot they now, these honours rare,
  This royal pomp and state ?
Can they restore the dead to life,
  Or close the scroll of Fate ?

Can they recall the early days—
    So joyous and so blest—
When France's gay and sunny soil
    Her feet in gladness prest?
Through all the splendour and the glare,
    Which mark the gorgeous scene,
Who can forget the headsman's axe?
    The pale and bleeding Queen?

And *thou*, stern Queen, whose jealous hate
    Thus ruthlessly could doom
The lovely rival of thy crown
    So early to the tomb ;
If ever sigh from broken heart
    May dare against thee plead,
Beware ! lest thou, in life's last days,
    Seek mercy in thy need.

For more of Love, and more of Truth,
    Thy helpless victim knew,
Than ever thou, in all thy pride,
    Around thy throne might view.
'Tis not the rank nor yet the gold
    That can affection move,
A gentle mind and kindly heart
    Alone we learn to love.

NORTHAMPTON.

"The proud beauty of the Midlands."—PENNANT.

I STAND amid the moving crowds which throng each
busy street,
Where wagons, carts, and hucksters' stalls, in wild
confusion meet ;
And palefac'd toilers listless roam, and country
damsels stray ;
Or loud-tongued politicians blame the statesmen of
the day !
Here portly farmers speak of crops, or moot the
price of grain ;
There Crispin's sons, with bitter speech, of new
machines complain.
But few who play their daily part in each strange
scene of life,
E'er think that here the robber Dane and Saxon
met in strife.

Aye, where the hawkers vend their wares, and noisy
    urchins play,
To gloomy Thor, the savage Dane would bow him
    down and pray.
To pray—his battle axe still wet with Saxon
    maiden's blood—
To pray—where smoking ruins mark'd where once
    a church had stood—
To pray—while dark rob'd monks and nuns lay
    bleeding in each cell ;
And all around the sword and flame work'd War's
    own bloody spell.
Oh ! God be thank'd, these times are past, and
    England may in peace
Behold her glory, wealth, and strength, still ever-
    more increase.

And yet I fain would linger still, and with impulsive
    strain,
Recall the splendours of the past, and bid them live
    again :—
An endless train of noble forms slow pass before my
    sight,
The Monarch, Prince, and belted Earl, the Church-
    man and the Knight.
Again arise the castle walls, and from their turrets
    high,
The silken banners blazon forth, and angry foes defy.

On ev'ry lofty battlement the warders' helmets
    shine,
And archers, on their trusty bows, in watchfulness
    recline.

While slowly rings the vesper bell, or aged minstrels
    sing
The famous deeds in Palestine of England's lion-
    king ;
And high-born maidens cast their glance of tender-
  • ness and love
On gallant youths, who, for their smile, their skill
    in tournays prove.
Again the fiery chargers prance before the castle
    gate,
Where pages young, in doublets gay, for steel-clad
    nobles wait ;
And tease the burly serving man, or kiss the bashful
    maid,
Or tremble at a monkish scowl, though never word
    be said.

But, lo ! the dreams begin to fade, and other forms
    I view :
The young and noble Cavaliers, to throne and
    monarch true :

Again they raise the wine-cup high, and mirthful
    ditties troll,
Or drink a bumper to their king, and raise a groan
    for " Noll."
Away again—the fight is o'er, and all is flight and
    rout ;
The clash of swords, and shrieks, and cries, mix with
    the victor's shout :
The crimson flames shoot madly up, and terror
    pales each brow—
The star of Royal Charles has wan'd, and Cromwell
    triumphs now.

Away again—no more the curse of strife and civil
    war
Brings mourning to each peaceful home, and spreads
    distress afar ;
But smiling crowds, and waving flags, and joyous
    clanging bells,
And lusty cheers, and music strains, the march of
    triumph swells :
'Tis England's Queen—her country's pride—who
    rests upon her throne, *
Surrounded by her people's love secure in *that*
    alone.

* Her Majesty visited Northampton, 1844.

Oh ! contrasts strange, these epochs four—the fierce
   and cruel Sweyne—
The Lion-King—the hapless Charles—and England's
   darling Queen.

Oh ! that I could, with prophet eye, into the Future
   peer,
And gaze upon the glories which shall crown each
   coming year ;
When men shall cast away the brand, and hate and
   war shall cease,
And each shall join his fellowman in works of love
   and peace ;
When Want and Woe shall never more our land
   with sorrow stain,
But joyous smiles and lighten'd hearts shall banish
   care and pain ;
When men in thankfulness shall tread the bright
   and blooming sod,
And raise their souls in grateful prayer to bless the
   works of God.

QUEEN ELEANOR'S CROSS, GEDDINGTON.

At Geddington was formerly a royal seat, which stood in the Castle or Hall Close, north-east of the church. Here, in 1188, was held a council, or parliament, by Henry II., to raise money for an expedition to the Holy Land. Six years later, Richard I. of England, and William, King of Scotland, were here together on a Good Friday. The corpse of Queen Eleanor rested here, on its way from Harby, in Nottinghamshire, where she died, to its final resting-place in Westminster Abbey. One of the Crosses erected by Edward I. to her memory still stands in the centre of the village. It is a beautiful and richly-ornamented structure, and in a good state of preservation.

Toll—toll—with a long deep roll,
Sobs the bell, as, in cross and stole,
Prays the Priest for the dead Queen's soul ;
And silent groups of people meet
Within the quaint and narrow street,
To bend the knee, and bow the head,
In sorrow for the queenly dead.
While in the dark sepulchral aisle
Of weeping Mary's ancient pile,

The hooded monks slow count each bead,
Or in the cloisters ceaseless plead
That earthly sins be now forgiv'n,
And Edward's Dove find rest in heav'n ;
And soft and low the mass is sung,
And to and fro the censors swung,
As blazing tapers cast a glare,
On England's monarch mourning there :
Beside the bier he takes his stand,
And clasps his brow with trembling hand ;
While toll—toll—with a long deep roll,
The bell's sad knell rings through his soul.

Toll—toll—with a long deep roll,
As vain would he his grief control,
And gazing on the altar screen,
Seek holy hopes on which to lean.
For oh ! the pain, and oh ! the woe
Of losing those whose truth we know ;
To wander through the World alone,
Nor find repose in crown or throne !
Ah ! who like Her would dare again
Drink from his wound the poison stain,
And ever prove, in peace and strife,
A tender, loving, faithful wife ?
" My Eleanor," he whisp'ring sighs,
" Oh ! smile on me from yonder skies ; "

And as he pray'd, the place did seem
To change as in some passing dream :
The songs of angels met his ears,
With sounds of harps from brighter spheres,
And looking up, joy fill'd his soul,
No more heard he the slow sad toll.

Oh ! joy, joy, for again he saw
The idol of his heart once more ;
In robes of light She stood array'd,
And smiles o'er her calm features play'd ;
To him more holy seems she now,
Than with the crown upon her brow—
Aye, lovelier far than when in pride,
She nestled by his royal side.
He fain would speak, yet can but kneel—
A numbing silence seems to seal
His quiv'ring lips, as high above
She gently points with looks of love ;
And then dissolves the vision fair,
Till nought is left but empty air.
The monkish chaunt he hears again,
And, weeping, swells the solemn strain ;
He sees his nobles as they throng
The columns of the church among ;
While ever booms the slow deep roll—
Toll—toll—for Eleanor's soul.

THE SKELETON.

On Thursday, March 24th, 1859, some men whilst ploughing in Mr. Passmore's field, at Little Addington, turned up an adult human skeleton, the head of which was found placed near its feet. It was believed by many to belong to a woman, who, about nine years since, when in an advanced state of pregnancy, suddenly disappeared from Ringstead, the village where she resided; having left her home one evening for the purpose of meeting her paramour. She has never since been heard of although a reward of £200 was offered by government for adequate information concerning her, if proved to have been murdered. The person deceased went out to meet was strongly suspected of the foul deed, and was obliged to fly from the village from the dread of popular vengeance which was strongly excited against him. The place where the skeleton was found is about a mile from Ringstead. It was not deep in the soil; but it was the first time the land had been ploughed on for several years. The skeleton was ascertained to be that of a female.

COULD they but speak—these fleshless bones,
    So cold, so damp, and white—
Perchance the secret they might breathe
    Of some wild fearful night,

When darkness veil'd the rustic scene,
  And *Mercy* bow'd her head,
As *Guilt* struck down his victim frail,
  With hands all crimson red ;
And dug with eager, trembling haste,
  The lone unhallow'd grave,
To hide from *human* eyes the crime,
  And Punishment to stave.

How strange to gaze upon the skull,
  So grim and senseless now,
And think how once, Love, Hope, and Joy
  Might flash across its brow ;
To dream how once the eyeless holes
  Could in their gladness beam,
Or glisten at Affection's tone,
  Or weep at Sorrow's theme ;
To muse how once the heaving breast,
  All flushing warm with life,
Could throb with varied feelings deep,
  Of Peace, or Care, and Strife.

But these are gone, and thought alone
  May dare recall the Past,
With all its chequer'd fleeting scenes,
  And bliss too sweet to last.

Perchance some tender parent taught,
 In Childhood's careless years,
Her maiden lips to breathe with love
 Of infant hopes and fears.
And when in after years *he* came
 Her trusting heart to woo,
She listen'd to his earnest vows,
 And blindly deem'd him true.

Perhaps he was, till Passion's dream
 And stolen joys were o'er ;
Till all her charms, her yielding love,
 Could sway him never more.
Then came the burning bitter Pain,
 The soul-consuming Shame,
As, with a cold averted look,
 Her love he would disclaim.
Then came the night of wan Despair,
 Of tears that e'er would start,
As still she hop'd—but hop'd in vain :
 For black Hate fill'd his heart.

And stern resolve—and thoughts of dread—
 Came flashing o'er his mind ;
And demon whispers oft he heard,
 And promptings undefin'd.

How, when, or where, we may not know
    Aught of the hidden crime,
Save these few bones ; but we may trust
    To Conscience and to Time.
Nor rest or peace the murderer knows ;
    E'en sleep deserts his eye :
His life is one fierce throbbing pang,
    And yet he fears to DIE.

KETTERING CHURCH.

The Tower of the Church was erected about 1450; but many portions of the edifice are of an earlier date; and the building appears to have suffered much during the Civil Wars. Great terror existed in Kettering during the great Plague.

I pass beneath the olden porch of Kett'ring's stately
    pile,
And wander 'mid the oaken pews which line the
    lengthen'd aisle ;

I see each lofty pillar'd arch, each Chapel silent now,
But where, in other times, the Monks to saints each
    knee would bow,
'Mid tombs of Knights, of gentle Dames, of War-
    riors fierce and bold ;
Illum'd with richly mellow'd lights of purple and
    of gold,
Which gleam'd thro' storied windows high, of bright
    and gorgeous hue ;
While holy chaunts from trembling lips, would
    float the openings through.

I silent muse, and deem I view the long procession
    slow—
The silver censors, crucifix, and monkish pomp and
    show :
They fade, and, lo ! a white-hair'd Man, with deep
    and earnest tone,
Reads from the Holy Book of Life, and makes its
    blessings known,
As round the simple reading desk the anxious
    hearers throng,
Anathemas no more to fear, nor shrink from priestly
    wrong.
But this departs ; and, fierce and swift, the flames
    of Civil War
Dart wildly o'er the peaceful scene, and terror
    spread afar.

"Quick! quick!! the church doors bolt and bar—
 the loud alarum ring!
They come, they come! the Puritans! who fear
 not Church or King."
Their swords and pikes ring on the doors, they
 shake, they yield, they fall,
And grim-faced men, of iron mould, stride through
 the sacred hall.
With reckless zeal they hack and hew the monuments of stone—
The artist-dreamings of a Past that shall no more
 be known;
While storm-winds howl through broken panes, and
 lurid light'nings glare,
And mock the desolation caus'd by mortal frenzy
 there.

Another vision yet I see: the cloud has pass'd away;
" *The King has got his own again;* " the wand'ring
 minstrels play;
But, hush! amid the harmony, the wine, the song,
 and mirth,
A ghastly Shadow silent glides, and smites each
 child of earth.
"The Plague! the Plague!" Away they fly; but
 whither, whither, where?
In North and South, in East and West, the danger
 meets them there.

They rush within the holy walls, in penitence they
 fall,
And God beseech, with tears and sobs, for mercy on
 them all.

But all these dreamings have an end—I wake, and
 see the crowd,
The silken dress, the cotton gown, the humble and
 the proud ;
I mark the jewell'd fingers clasp the velvet book of
 prayer,
While horny hands turn over leaves, old, greasy,
 worn, and bare.
Yet Rich and Poor are all alike before the sight of
 God ;
Death waits on each, and bids them rest beneath
 the grassy sod,
And tells us not on earthly things to place our
 sympathies,
But learn a lesson from the Past, its hopes, and
 fears, and sighs.

THE ANCIENT READING-DESK IN KETTERING CHURCH.

After the Reformation, the use of the Bible was allowed to the people, and orders were issued by Henry VIII. that one should be placed in every place of worship, for public perusal; but, such was the value of a printed book in those days, that each volume was securely attached, by means of chains, to the reading desk. One of these desks is preserved in Kettering church, with the chains still fastened to the covers of a Bible and Fox's Book of Martyrs. Over the porch of the church is a small stone chamber, supposed to have formerly been the abode of the "morrow mass priest" and his attendant, whose duty was "to sing masses for ever and ever" in the chauntry chapel, still existing.

Look on this desk, so plain and bare,
　Look on its rusty chains,
Look on the covers rotting there,
　Defac'd with age and stains.
Perchance it seems but worthless *now*,
　But not so deem'd the crowd,
Which cluster'd round the aged priest,
　Who read The Book aloud.
No more for priestly pomp and show
　Their simple hearts might care ;
Of greater value to them seem'd
　That Desk, so plain and bare.

Ah ! never did the Fathers deem,
  As they each mass did say,
Or slowly chaunt the choral psalm,
  Or to the Virgin pray,
How soon the hallow'd star of Truth
  Should in its glory shine,
And swift disperse the clouds and gloom
  Which darken'd Mercy's shrine.
Oh ! Freedom hath her relics, which
  She guards with saintly care ;
But none in worth may e'er surpass
  That Desk, so plain and bare.

Aye, there it stands—look on it now,
  And scorn it if thou will ;
Nor let the flame of Liberty
  Within thy bosom thrill !
But unto us will it recall
  That bright and glorious time,
When Luther burst the chains of Rome,
  And preach'd the Truth sublime.
Let heroes have their monuments
  Of marble, chaste and fair ;
But nobler is that relic old—
  That Desk, so plain and bare.

SIMON DE ST. LIZ.

Simon de St. Liz was the son of Randoel le Ryche, who came over with William the Conqueror. William wished the Countess Judith, the widow of Waltheof, first Earl of Northampton, to marry Simon, but she refused on account of his lameness; but the king soon afterwards gave him her daughter Maude in marriage. The union was celebrated with great pomp and splendour; and about 1084 Simon and Maude richly endowed the various churches and religious establishments of the town and county. Maude appears to have been instrumental in changing the fierce nature of her warrior husband, who built Fotheringhay castle to do her honour, and afterwards went to the Holy Land, in the time of Henry I., and was even commencing a second pilgrimage to the Holy Sepulchre when he died, and was buried within the walls of the Abbey of St. Mary of Charity, in France. After his death, Maude became the wife of David, king of Scotland, whose descendants inherited her estates.

Lord Simon was the bravest knight
   In Norman William's train;
He never shrank from foe in fight,
   Or rais'd his sword in vain.

His brow was mark'd with seam and scar
  His wounds had made him lame ;
Yet brilliant feats of chivalry
  Had brought him wealth and fame.

Lord Simon ne'er had bow'd his knee
  At Love's own gentle shrine ;
And brighter than a Maiden's smile
  To him seem'd War and Wine.

" Ho ! ho !"—laugh'd William to his knights—
  " No heirs will Simon see,
Unless a maid for him be sought,
  That he may wedded be."

Then each fair damsel blush'd and smil'd ;
  But Judith's eyes flash'd fire ;
Her cheek was pale with hate and scorn ;
  Her soul was fill'd with ire.

" Keep back your Norman wolves, or, Man !
  Beware the tigress' spring !
I will not wed the man I hate
  At beck of Bastard King ! "

King William frown'd.   Lord Simon glar'd ;
  Then grasp'd his axe and sword,
And would have sworn a fearful curse
  But for the gentle Maude ;

Who knelt her down before the King :
   "Oh ! Sire, my parent spare,
And let me be the sacrifice ;
   I, Simon's fate will share."

Lord Simon bow'd his head, and said ;
   " A soldier's words are few ;
But here's my hand, and here's my heart ;
   Both, like my sword, are true."

" And though my nature may be rough,
   More fit for war than play,
I bring with me an earnest love   .
   That shall not pass away."

The bells were rung, the dance and song
   Commingled with the wine ;
And loud the toasts went gaily round,
   And bright each eye did shine :

While pennons flutter'd in the breeze,
   And helms and lances shone,
As. at the Altar, Simon claimed
   His bride for him alone.

Where flows the calm and placid Nene,
   Through fields of waving grain,
Lord Simon built his castle home,
   To guard his wide domain.

And he would speak of knightly deeds—
    Of battles lost and won ;
Of Saxon strongholds storm'd and burnt ;
    Yet smile fair Maude had none :

For pious Nuns had train'd her heart
    To things of peace and love ;
And when he prais'd the victor's march,
    Her heart with grief would move.

He could not chide, nor yet reprove,
    For, oh ! her tearful glance
Had touch'd his stern and warlike soul,
    And bade him leave his lance—

Aye, lance and sword, and axe and shield,
    With armour, plumes and all,
To rot and rust amid the dust
    Below the castle hall.

And sadly musing on the past,
    . He mourn'd the murder'd slain :—
" Oh, Christ ! have mercy on my soul,
    I touch not sword again :

But bow me down before Thy Cross,
    In penitence sincere ;
For more than deadly grasp of foe
    Thy anger, Lord, I fear."

Ah! dear to Maude seem'd Simon then,
  And smiles adorn'd her brow,
As with a joyous pride she spake :—
  " I *love* thee, Simon, *now ;*

Not all my lands, not all my gems,
  My servants, or my gold,
Can ever be more dear to me
  Than thou, my husband bold."

He fondly led her by the arm,
  And wander'd down the grove ;
Nor dream'd again of War and Fame,
  But clung to Peace and Love.

The years roll'd by, and holy fanes
  With wealth had they endow'd ;
Reliev'd the poor ; and taught the great
  Their duties to the crowd.

The people learnt their names to bless,
  And priests for them to pray ;
Nor once did Simon's heart regret
  The sword he flung away.

But in the fulness of his heart,
  He long'd to view the shrine,
Where pilgrims bow'd, and fervent pray'd,
  In distant Palestine.

He parted from his darling Maude ;
    Down dropp'd her trembling hands :
Alas ! she never saw him more—
    He died in foreign lands.

No monument of brass or stone
    Records his life or fame ;
No earthly things like these we need
    To save an Hero's name.

THE SUICIDE.

The circumstances on which these lines were founded occurred at Bozeat, and afforded a painful instance of mischief arising from the prevalency of an impaired state of morals amongst the labouring population of our country districts.

FROM the water raise the Maiden,
    Gather up her dripping hair,
Glossy once, and neatly braiden
    O'er her brow so white and fair.
Shrink not from her as she, lying
    On the damp and chilly grass,
Wears the look she wore when dying,
    As the dream of Life did pass.

Blame her not, but strive to borrow
  Mercy from thy brighter fame ;
Kindly judge of Ellen's sorrow,
  Of her agony and shame.
Think of her with heart all broken,
  By a faithless love betray'd,
Ev'ry vow once fondly spoken
  False as he who had them made.

Oh ! the days of mortal anguish,
  The repentance and the pain,
As in loneness she would languish
  For her innocence again !
Oh ! the dread of scorn and laughter,
  Haunting her by night and day
Till she feared not Death's hereafter,
  As she cast her life away !

With no heed of flowers springing,
  In the woodland, grove, or lea ;
Nor of Nature's warblers' singing,
  'Mid the branches of each tree.
Earth has lost its sunny brightness,
  All is terror, clouds and gloom ;
And her spirit's early lightness
  Sinks beneath her Sorrow's doom.

From the homestead see her flying,
   With her flush'd and burning cheek,
With her heart e'er inward sighing
   Of the grief she might not speak.
See her by the silent water,
   Clench'd her lips, and clasp'd her hands,
In her madness—wretched daughter !—
   Lost in dread resolve she stands.

See her eyelids—how they quiver !
   See the teardrops burning fall ;
See her form in terror shiver,
   As she breathes farewell to all.
Then in desperation leaping
   With no thought or care beyond
The wish to end her earthly weeping
   In the lone and dreary pond.

SIR FRANCIS TRESHAM.

Rushton Hall was founded by Sir Thomas Tresham, about 1595.
Many traditionary legends are associated with it, and also with
the curious Triangular Lodge, situated in Rushton Park.
One remarkable circumstance connected with the latter building
is that everything is TRINE, or threefold! This has led to a
supposition that it was intended to be symbolical of the Trinity.
Sir Thomas Tresham was cruelly persecuted for his adherence
to the faith of the Roman Church; and when he died, in 1605,
his son Francis was easily induced, from the remembrance of
the injuries he had endured, to enter into the Gunpowder Plot.
The result is known to all. The conspirators were either
arrested, or saved themselves by flight. Tresham was among
the former, and was committed to the Tower, where he perished
—according to popular belief—by poison, on the 23rd Dec.,
1606. It would seem that at this period all parties had lost
sight of the principles which constitute TRUE Christianity, and
hence the hatred and persecution inflicted by either side.

DECEMBER 25th, 1605.

THE Christmas chimes peal'd sweetly forth from
    Rothwell's sacred fane,
As Tresham gaz'd, with listless eye, o'er Rushton's
    snow-wrapt plain;

And silent mus'd, with burning heart—with passions fierce and strong—

How once his faith had been upheld by Sword, by
Law, and Song :

While now its very name was plac'd beneath the
vengeful ban

Of men who, in the name of *Christ*, enforc'd the
laws of *man* ;

And hunted those who once, in pride, made rulers
kneel as slaves,

But now lay trembling in their cells, or lifeless in
their graves.

He dreamt of masses chaunted slow, in tones of
grief and fear,

In cellars dark—in vaults and caves—where foemen
might not hear,

Or view the careworn, weeping few, who, with the
nerve of old,

Preferr'd to cling to Cross and Stole, and lose their
earthly gold.

And as he mus'd a troubled look came flashing o'er
his brow ;

His fingers sought the rapier's hilt.   Why starts he
backward now ?

Hark ! Hark ! He hears the peasant's voice in
strains of gladness sing

The grateful carol of his heart to earth's Eternal King.

Down—down—ye dreams of blood and strife, begone
　　ye thoughts of dread,
Let not the Joy-day of the year be stain'd with
　　murder red.
If evil dreamings still *will* rise within thy busy
　　brain,
Take counsel, Man, and think of Him in lowly man-
　　ger lain ;
Who came to bless our hearts with faith ; our souls
　　with zeal to move ;
And teach us not to *slay* our foes, but conquer them
　　with love,
Nor breathe the lust of Hate and Scorn, nor Fury's
　　evil ban,
But kindly herald " Peace on Earth," and sing
　　. " Good-will to man."

DECEMBER 25th, 1606.

A blacken'd corse lies stark and cold within the
　　gloomy walls
That silent frown on stately Thames, amid the
　　snow that falls
In countless flakes, on hulls and masts—on boats
　　and barges grim,
Which, in the mist, glide o'er the waves, like spectral
　　fancies dim :

And this the end of all the Toil, the Dreamings, and
    the Strife !

The crimson'd rack, the poison'd draught ; a form
    devoid of life !

A name for ever stained with shame—a nation's
    bitter hate—

And talents lost, which, but for this, had made
    their owner great.

Again the bells of Christmas peal their sounds of
    joy and mirth,

And strive, for once, to hush the clang of Hate and
    War on earth ;

To stay the din of rival creeds, the aims of priest
    and king,

And to the regions of the past their ceaseless
    struggles fling.

But, lo ! this corse, these frowning guards, these
    sounds of sword and spear

Arise, as though they fain would mock the welcome
    strains we hear ;

But even yet the Emblem springs, e'en from the
    bloody dust,

That never cause may dare succeed by means that
    are not just.

THE DEATH BRIDAL.

Founded on a tragical incident which occured at Kettering, December 25th, 1858; when a young man—an acquaintance of the author—committed suicide on the morning of his intended marriage. He had taken some rooms, and furnished them; but not making his appearance at his sweetheart's home, the door of his room was broken open, when he was discovered lying lifeless on the bed, with a miniature of his betrothed and an open prayer book before him, and a recently discharged pistol on the floor. The report of the deadly weapon was heard by the neighbours as the Waits were playing the Christmas Carol near the house. The real cause of the fatal deed never transpired.

THE Bride awaits her loving Lord :
   Why lingers he so long ?
The time is past—yet comes he not
   To join the festive throng !
Ah ! little dost thou dream, poor Girl,
   Of what thou soon must know ;
That thou must change thy bridal dress,
   For Sorrow's garb of woe !
Aye, from thy fair and maiden brow
   Tear down thy bridal wreath—
Thy hopes are dash'd—thy dreams are flown—
   Thy Lover sleeps in death !

H

With bleeding brow, and blacken'd hands—
　　With limbs all stiff and stark—
In chamber lone his corse repos'd,
　　That morning cold and dark ;
The Christmas chimes were pealing loud,
　　And homes with joy were glad :
Oh! who might dare, this day of mirth,
　　To murmur and be sad ?
But never in our cup of bliss
　　Is drop without alloy ;
And seldom may we dare to dream
　　But griefs our dreams destroy.

And thou, poor Girl, thy tears are vain :
　　No more may he return
To bless with joy thy youthful heart,
　　Which now but lives to mourn.
With smile serene upon his lips—
　　He cold and lifeless lies,
No more to feel thy tender kiss,
　　Or hear thy sweet replies ;
And thou may'st weep, and thou may'st cry,
　　In anguish wild, forlorn ;
The sunshine of thy promis'd bliss
　　From thee for aye hath gone.

'Twas *thee* he lov'd, for *thee* he liv'd ;
 He thought of *thee* in death ;
Thy pictur'd form alone beheld
 Thy Lover's parting breath.
Oh ! who may dare depict the pain,
 The anguish and despair,
Which wrung his warm and ardent soul,
 And pierc'd his heart with care ;
Till reason left her shaking throne,
 And Madness came to guide
The uprais'd arm—and fatal aim—
 Of Frank, the suicide.

Slow bear him to the church yard green,
 Slow pace the grassy sod ;
Nay, tremble not, poor weeping Bride,
 But trust and hope in God :
Heark'n to the words of peace and faith-
 Of calm and holy trust—
With which thy Lover's lifeless form
 Returns as dust to dust.
Alas ! thou canst not still thy grief :
 With pain thy breast doth swell ;
Thy limbs grow faint—earth seems to fade—
 Love—Husband—Frank—farewell !

THE LEGEND OF BURLEIGH HOUSE.

———

One of the most beautiful legends connected with the manorial
  residences of our nobility, is that of Burleigh House. It has
  ever been a favourite theme for poets, and some of the best
  verses of Tennyson and Moore are founded on the subject.
  The more exciting traditions of olden time may pass away and
  be forgotten, but the affecting narrative of Lord Burleigh and
  the Cottager's daughter will ever remain graven on the hearts
  of those who have once heard it; and it will always--to use
  the words of a Quarterly Reviewer—"form one of the finest
  pages of romance in the British Peerage."

———

THE Lord of Burleigh walketh slow,
　　With grave and sadden'd air,
In the park, and pleasant garden   .
　　Around his mansion fair.
The Summer sun, with golden shine,
　　Gilds tree, and shrub, and flower ;
The fountain bright ; the sculpture rare ;
　　The grove and shady bower :
But all their beauties tempt in vain
　　The weary heart of *him*
Who museth of a happy Past
　　Ere eyes with tears were dim :

Ere he had lost his Lily sweet—
    The fairest, heart might see ;
For whom he could his fortune yield,
    Nor Lord of Burleigh be.

Oh ! happy, happy, happy time,
    When—clad in lowly guise—
Unknown he left his stately halls,
    To seek the smiling eyes
Of one who lov'd him for *himself*,
    And not his rank or gold ;
A soul to whom his own could breathe
    Its yearnings manifold.
And such a one to him became
    His darling hope and pride ;
The list'ner of his earnest vows,
    His young and lovely Bride.
But never, in her wildest dreams,
    Or strangest fancies free,
She deem'd that he who claim'd her love,
    Could Lord of Burleigh be !

He led her from the Cottage home,
    From ev'ry olden tie,
That she might share his lowly fate—
    With him succeed or die.
He led her to his stately hall—
    The secret still his own—

And told her that Lord Burleigh lov'd,
   And lov'd but her alone !
" No ! no !--she cried, and sobbing knelt—
   " His love I do not need ;
So that thou but remain with me,
   My heart is rich indeed."
He smil'd, and rais'd her gently up—
   Each servant bow'd the knee—
" Look up, Fond Heart, and in thy Love,
   The Lord of Burleigh see ! "

Transplanted Lilies seldom thrive,
   They love their native glade ;
Beneath the warmth of sunnier skies,
   The fairest Snowdrops fade.
And though she lov'd the titled *Lord*,
   As best a bride became ;
That Lord when clad in lowly garb,
   A fonder love could claim.
She spurn'd as dross the shining gold,
   And priz'd as wealth the Mind ;
What wonder that in Burleigh's heart
   Her form should dwell enshrin'd !
Although within the marble tomb,
   Her earthly shape may be—
Although no more her peaceful smile,
   The Lords of Burleigh see !

THE DYING SOLDIER.

Not a few of those brave-hearted soldiers who died amid the pestilential marshes of Varna, or during the Crimean struggle, or in attempting to reduce the rebellious population of India, were born and reared in Northamptonshire homes; and in many a lonely dwelling there is reverently preserved some hallowed little relic—of small value in itself, but precious from the associations connected with it; and the mother's eyes will glisten as she relates the old tale of her poor noble hearted boy, who perished while defending with his life the cause of his country. One case of this nature was that of a young man, named Alfred Marriott, of Kettering, who died at Allahabad, from the effects of wounds received whilst in action against the Indian rebels. He possessed in a great degree the sacred fire of genuine poetry; and it is to be regretted that he preferred to exchange the poet's pen for the sword and a soldier's death in a far off land. Such is Glory.

WHERE Gauges' waters silent roll in beauty sweet
    and calm;
And Indian temples proudly smile from stately
    groves of palm,
A wounded soldier dying lay, and writh'd in mor-
    tal pain;
His eye was dim, his cheek was pale, and moist with
    crimson stain.

No mother's love, no sister's care, in that far land
    he knew ;
But near his dying couch he saw the fierce and
    stern Hindoo. ·
He saw the burning glance of Hate e'er watch his
    gasping breath ;
He saw the hands that long'd to clutch, and strangle
    him to death.
He shudder'd as his eye he clos'd, and dream'd of
    home again—
The grassy meads, the rural lanes, the daisy-span-
    gled plain ;
The ancient church ; his cottage home, the sports
    of early days ;
And in his trance no more he fear'd the Hindoo's
    vengeful gaze.

No more he strode 'mid rebel hordes, 'mid scenes of
    carnage dread ;
No more he heard the vultures' scream where lay
    the ghastly dead.
No burning jungle staid him now, his path was
    straight and clear ;
He trod again his native town, and clasp'd the
    forms so dear ;

He heard the happy, peaceful chimes of distant
    village bells,
And roam'd Northampton's shady groves, and lone
    romantic dells ;
Or stroll'd down lordly avenues, or from the brow
    of hill
Would gaze upon the fields below, or on the rustic
    mill ;
He saw the reapers at their toil, bind up the golden
    sheaves,
Or rest them from the noontide sun beneath the
    shady leaves ;
While laughing children frolic'd by, and swallows
    clove the air,
And manly forms, with earnest tone, commun'd
    with maidens fair.

He saw again his childhood's home, more dear unto
    him *now*
Than all the gorgeous palaces which India's clime
    may show ;
And in that home he deem'd he view'd the object of
    his love :
His heart was full, his breast glow'd warm, his soul
    with joy did move :

With open arms he forward rush'd to meet the
    maiden fair,
When, lo ! the start dispell'd his dream—he clasp'd
    but empty air !
A bitter sigh escap'd his lips, a low half-mutter'd
    prayer ;
And, with his hands cross'd on his breast, alone he
    perish'd there.
They plac'd his form in simple grove, unmark'd by
    cross or stone,
And soon the very place itself to all will be un-
    known.
Oh, England ! spare one tear for these brave hearts,
    though poor they be ;
They sacrifice Home, Blood, and Life, that thou
    may'st aye be free.

THE FATAL DUEL.

Sir James Enyon was Lord of the Manor, of Floore, in the time of Charles I., and was slain in a duel with Sir Nicholas Crispe. According to Baker, the Northamptonshire Historian, " both parties were volunteers in the royal cause, and the dispute arose at their quarters in Gloucestershire. The fatal result made an indelible impression on the mind of the survivor, who ever after wore mourning, except on the field of battle, when he cherished the hope of being united to his friend by a fortunate bullet; and through life hallowed every return of the melancholy anniversary by closing his chamber in darkness, and devoting himself to fasting and prayer."

For many, many years, in friendship sweet,
    Had their young hearts commingled as but one;
Nor felt the baneful glow of Passion's heat
    Their truth assail, or change their earnest tone,
    As soul commun'd with soul on terrace lone,
Where on the twain, the Star of Evening pale
    Would gently smile from its high azure throne ;
While softly sang the hidden nightingale,
Amid the leafy boughs of the surrounding vale.

But, lo ! the flame of fierce rebellion spread,
    Swift circling over England's peaceful land ;
Whose grassy plains would echo with the tread
    Of Puritans, or fiery Rupert's band,
      Who, for their king, would wave each gleaming
        brand ;
Nor did Sir James, nor Crispe, his friend, restrain
    The zeal they felt, but fearless chose to stand
Amid the few, who strove—but strove in vain—
To raise the fallen throne of hapless Charles again,

One eve—one fatal eve—they deeply drank ;
    And strife was kindled at some fancied slight :
Till Love gave way to Hate, and neither shrank
    To meet each other in the hostile fight :
      And as their swords they cross'd, the flashes
        bright
Shone quiv'ring in the pale gray beams of morn,
    Which cast o'er each a wild unearthly light,
And stern illum'd the bitter glance of scorn,
And the proud heaving breasts with angry passions
    torn.

No sweet remembrance of the Past might swell
    Their souls within, and reconcile the twain,
But fierce and fast the sword-thrusts pass'd, till fell
    The Lord of smiling Floore, on dew damp plain ;

Then knelt Sir Nicholas, and rav'd in vain ;
　And beat his breast, and weeping, bow'd his head
　　In grief and sorrow for the murder'd slain ;
Nor rest he more might know, for round his bed
At night would ghastly phantoms shriek, "He's
　　　dead—dead—dead."

With haggard face he sought his monarch's camp,
　And in the fray was e'er the foremost seen ;
The first to hear the foeman's stealthy tramp,
　　The last to leave the blood-stain'd battle scene ;
　　For e'er he thought with mortal anguish keen,
Of dying Enyon, who, with trembling sigh,
　　Forgave the murd'rer's deed, and smil'd serene ;
Till Crispe would clasp his hands, and madly cry
In his remorse, aloud, and long that he might die.

But, ah ! no bullet swift, nor gleaming blade,
　Could end his sad career of pain and woe ;
In penitence he sought the gloomy shade
　　Where he was born and rear'd, and taught to
　　　know
　　The chequer'd follies of Life's pomp and show,
And here in peace he pray'd to be forgiven
　　By Him who bids the seasons come and go ;
And when at length the threads of life were riven,
With hands cross'd on his breast, he, dying, look'd
　　　to Heaven.

NASEBY.

" The site of the battle is a wide and long stretch of ground, with
a gentle slope from the northern and southern extremities to
the lower space between, about one mile north of the village.
There are some depressions in the field, but it is not generally
broken, though somewhat of its ruggedness is now probably
worn off. At the time of the fight it was an open heath, and
remained, until the present century, a rough undulating stretch
of high moorland, covered with gorse and fern, and scattered
bramble bushes."—WHELAN. The fight commenced with a
forlorn hope of three hundred Roundheads, who advanced
towards the Royal army, but were charged by Prince Rupert,
and driven back with great loss, their leader, Ireton, being made
prisoner. Rupert and his followers pursued their foes for a
great distance; but, on returning, found that Cromwell and his
Ironsides had gained the field, and that the King had fled in
the direction of Leicester. Many relics of the conflict—
such as sword hilts, cannon balls, &c.—are still occasionally
dug up by the spade of the farm labourer.

On the sloping ridge of the Moorland, where
   The Furze blossoms shone in the blithe June morn,
The Royalists stood with a fearless air,
   And gaz'd on their foes with a smile of scorn ;

Till the Roundheads frown'd, and their fingers
        clench'd
    The hilts of their swords with a close tight hold—
The grasp of an Hate, which ne'er would be quench'd
    Till the red blood stream'd on the hill side mould.

The gay banners wav'd in the morning breeze,
    With the pride and pomp of a happier day;
Yet long ere the night wind sigh'd through the trees,
    All crimson'd and torn, on the grass they lay.
But, hark! to that shout, and the quick firm tramp
    Of the grim-fac'd men, in their corslets bright,
As they fearless march to the Monarch's camp,
    With their stout arms nerv'd for the last dread
        fight.

"What? Ho! Rupert, quick! To horse, Prince, away!
    On the foemen's helms let thy sword strokes ring—
See! Ireton, himself, leads on to the fray—
    Now, Prince, do thy best for thy own true King!"
No more! but away! lo! the war steeds swept
    With a light'ning speed to the plain below;
And the riders' hearts with a stern glow leapt,
    As before them stood—like a wall—the foe.

With a loud wild shout, and the fierce sharp thrust
    Of their own keen swords, they gallantly spring
On the Roundheads' ranks; and down to the dust,
    With a curse, the flower of their foes they fling.

Through the green corn fields—through the lone-
    some wood—   .
The Cavaliers swift in the War-chase ride,
Till their spurs are moist with the foam and blood
From the quiv'ring flesh of each courser's side.

High the bright sun shone with a rich warm glare,
    As th' Royalists paus'd in their reckless speed,
To heark'n to the cry which thrill'd through the air ;
    "Back, back to your King, in his sad dire need."
Again, back again, with their blades still red,
    Back, back to the field, where the Roundheads'
      brand
With a Victor march had in triumph sped—
    The Prince, with a shout, darts on with his band.

Too late ! for the King, with his train, has flown
    From the blood stain'd field, a fugitive poor,
In the land where erst his crown and his throne,
    In their strength and pow'r, seem'd for aye secure.
Too late ! and the heart of the proud Prince falls ;
    And his eyes are moist with the salt, salt tears ;
With a loud wild cry for his King he calls,
    But the victor's hymn is all that he hears.

BOUGHTON HOUSE.

This palatial mansion is one of the residences of the Duke of
Buccleuch, and is situate about two miles from Kettering. It
was originally erected by Ralph, Duke of Montague; and the
traces of its original grandeur are still to be found in the
splendid terrace on the principal front, and in the canal, nearly
a mile in length, which runs through the park. The subjoined
Ode was written at the urgent request of several of the Duke's
tenantry, on the occasion of the marriage of his eldest son, the
Earl Dalkeith, with the Lady Louisa Hamilton, Nov. 10, 1859.

RECITATIVE.

THOUGH sombre, dark, and cheerless dawn
The wintry, cold, November morn ;
Still Joy shall chase the gloom away,
And acclamations hail the day—
The day which views the loving pride
With which young Dalkeith claims his bride,
And clasps her to his noble breast,
In her affection wrapt and blest ;

E'en I—a lowly Bard—would fain
Awake my harp's responsive strain,
And for a bridal garland bring
The simple verses which I sing.

SONG.

Gone, gone are the knightly days of old,
 When the Minstrel Harpers sang ;
When the Grey Monks left their beads untold,
 To list to the cheers which rang
From the lusty throats of warders brave—
 To their Chieftain leal and true—
As, bowing the knee, they welcom'd home
 The Bride of the bold Buccleuch.

The claymore is sheath'd, the bucklers swing
 In peace from the oaken wall ;
No more the clash of the lances ring
 From turret, from roof, and hall.
Flown are the dreams of chivalry bright,
 And flown are their glories too ;
No more will the bronze-fac'd champions hail
 The Bride of the bold Buccleuch.

RECITATIVE.

But why should I thus sad prolong
The notes of my impulsive song,

In mournful wailings for the past,
As though the things of earth could last?
Away, ye thoughts : let happier strains
Awake the echoes of the plains.

SONG.

In the rich fond warmth of thy maiden heart,
  Young Bride, nestle close to thy fond love's side,
For ne'er shall his soul refuse to impart
  Its truth, or its love, to his own sweet Bride.
Hark ! hark to the cheer !—to the cheer which swells
  From the Highland crags—from the Lowland
    plains—
From the smiling homes of the English dells,
  Where Contentment lives, and Happiness reigns ;
And hark to the peal of the dancing chimes,
  That merrily ring from the belfry old,
With the welcomes rare of the simple times
  When a heart was dear, dearer far than gold.

CHORUS.

  No empty tributes do we bring ;
  No idle praises do we sing :
  But with a welcome, fond and true,
  We hail the Bride of young Buccleuch.

SONG.

Like the snow-white buds which graceful entwine
 In a circling wreath on thy lovely brow,
May the roseate hopes of the Future shine,
 E'er as brightly and smiling as now.
May never storm-cloud o'er thy Life-path frown,
 Or the glory dim of thy heart's sunshine ;
May never a grief on thy soul weigh down,
 Or rend with a pang, the fair breast of thine ;
May the golden smile of a summer day,
 When the blossoms thrill with their sweet perfume,
Be the emblem rare of thy young life's way,
 In the radiant sphere where the heart-joys bloom·

CHORUS.

No empty tributes do we bring ;
No idle praises do we sing :
But with a welcome, fond and true,
We hail the Bride of young Buccleuch.

ROCKINGHAM CASTLE.

A SONNET.

————

The Castle is erected on a stately eminence, which overlooks
the grassy vale of the Welland; and in former times it
consisted of a large keep, defended with double-embattled
walls, and numerous towers, of which the two bastions which
flanked the gateway are the only parts now remaining. Con-
siderable historical interest is attached to the fortress, which
was formerly a favourite resort of the early English Sovereigns.
The present mansion is situate in the courtyard. A flower
show is annually held here, when the noble terraces, spacious
lawns, and beautiful gardens are thrown freely open to the
public.

————

Far better thus—that, 'neath the ancient trees,
   The archway grim, or on each terrace wide,
   Where warriors oft have fought, and bled, and died,
These smiling groups should breathe the summer
      breeze,
Sweet laden with perfumes from grassy leas,
   From woodland groves, or streamlet's mossy side,
   Than that the reckless dreams of blood and pride,
Should all our noblest aspirations sieze :

For it must surely be a holier aim
To emulate in arts of Peace, nor claim
The dubious honours of the field of strife,
  Where War lifts up on high the crimson'd wreath,
And twines it round the shrinking brows of Life,
  Which homage yields unto its victor—Death !

THORPE MALSOR.

Thorpe Malsor is a pretty little village, situate about two miles
from Kettering, and the seat of the Maunsell family. A curious
legend is extant of one of their ancestors, who fought at the
battle of Naseby, and was wounded and left for dead. The
body was about to be stripped preparatory to burial, when a
young woman, the daughter of an apothecary, happened to be
on the field, and finding his hand to be very soft, exclaimed—
" This certainly was a gentleman." She further observed that
she felt a pulse, and consequently, that he was not dead. She
put off her petticoat, and wrapping him in it, had him conveyed
to a neighbouring village, where he recovered. Mr. Maunsell,
being thus providentially rescued from death, lived for some
years afterwards, and employed the young woman as a
housekeeper, till the time of his death, when he left her a
handsome annuity.

Long have I known the fierce and restless throb
  Of smoke-dried teeming Cities, where
Is often heard the low and wailing sob
  Of Labour mourning in despair—

Where many-___ ___d Fact'rics sternly frown,
    Like sullen _____ coldly grim ;
Where Steam, to mighty engines harness'd down,
    E'er booms proud Mammon's triumph hymn—
Till my poor weary heart was flush'd and stir'd,
    And would no more—Slave-like—be driven ;
But rather, as some wounded flutt'ring bird,
    Aye sought to wing its flight to Heaven.

But *now* I tread the soft and grassy plain,
    Or seek the woodland's solitude ;
Or in the lone and silent country lane,
    Feel all my soul with joy imbued :
While in my breast a thousand fancies throng
    Fond nestling there like some young dove,
Till, with a burst, they ripen into song—
    The strains of high immortal love.
A love which fain would rouse men's sympathies
    To nobler, brighter, purer themes,
Than those which clog their minds with soulless ties,
    And prove but vain and fleeting dreams.

And here, fair Thorpe, hath my young soul divin'd
    The subtle secret of the spheres ;
How kindred thoughts and feelings ever bind
    In one fond link, which life endears,

The humble Toiler's aspirations pure
  With those his richer brethren feel ;
To sing the mortal ills which men endure,
  And strive their sufferings to heal.
For false are those base slaves whose tongues e'er dare
  To breathe the cold and senseless lie—
That Rich and Poor for each can *never* care,
  But in their hatred, aye, must die !

Oh ! dearest Thorpe, my thoughts are link'd with
    thee !
  And ever in my dreams I view
Thy winding walks, thy groves, and grassy lea—
  For ever old, yet ever new.
I love thee for the mem'ries sweet and blest,
  With which I shrine thy simple name
Within this lowly heart which knew not rest
  Till thou its love had sought to claim.
May ne'er the Vandal hand of change efface
  Thy smiling charms—thy beauties rare—
Or rob thy blooming landscape of its grace—
  A grace which time itself could spare.

MISCELLANEOUS POEMS.

.

MISCELLANEOUS POEMS.

HERBERT ARLE.

DEAR Sister, raise me gently up, and ope the case-
  ment wide,
  That I may view the narrow path which winds
  across the lea,
For Herbert Arle has fondly said that I shall be his
  bride,
  And to-day, to-day he's coming, he's coming unto
  me.

They told me that another form, with tender vows,
  he woo'd,
  And my poor soul too soon, alas! the lying tale
  believ'd,
Till in my bitter wretchedness and agony I rued
  The hour in which my plighted troth I fancied
  was deceiv'd.

But it was false—so Herbert says—from me he
    never rov'd,
  Although he left his father's home to cross the
    foamy sea,
Still never for a moment I by him was unbelov'd,
  And to-day, to-day he's coming, he's coming back
    to me.

Pray draw the little curtains back, and place the
    fuschia where
  So oft I used to stand and watch in loneliness for
    him,
Till weary with my vigil drear I sank into the chair,
  My young heart anxious with its doubts, my eyes
    with weeping dim.

From yonder shelf, dear, reach me down that Testa-
    ment of mine,
  It was my Herbert's birthday gift—inside behold
    his name,
And as he placed it in my hands he said, "While
    stars should shine
  His heart to me would ever be in constancy the
    same."

What right had I to doubt his word, or for a mo-
    ment fear
  That he to love, or thrice-told vow, could e'er a
    traitor be?

There was no cause for me to shed a single sigh or
    tear,
  For to-day, to-day he's coming, he's coming back
    to me.

Girl, do I look so very thin? my cheek so very pale?
  My eye so sunken and so bright? Nay, do not
    turn away!
'Tis false! I'm getting well again, and soon we'll
    roam the vale,
  As in the happy, joyous time, when we could
    romp and play.

And you shall be my bridesmaid, dear; white
    blossoms we will wear,
  They'll look so pretty and so nice, with Herbert
    by my side;
Oh! how the village gossips old will ope their eyes
    and stare,
  As from the ivy cover'd church my Herbert leads
    his bride.

Fair Autumn's sunny splendours glint the forests
    grand and old,
  Where leafy branches softly surge like ripples on
    the sea;
The joy-hopes of my stricken heart again their wings
    unfold,
  For to-day, to-day he's coming, he's coming back
    to me,

See there he is, just by the stile, beneath the syca-
　　more :
　　But who is that whom thus he leads with loving,
　　　　gentle care ?
Methinks I've seen that flaunting dress and coquette
　　air before !
　　She turns her head—I know her now—my rival,
　　　　Alice Clare !

I see it all—they sought to mock my misplac'd
　　foolish love,
　　To trample on my outrag'd soul, and triumph in
　　　　my pain ;
But they, poor fools, may scarcely know how strong
　　the heart can prove,
　　How, crush'd and bleeding, it can rise and laugh
　　　　in proud disdain.

But for this slight, no scorn had fill'd this woman's
　　breast of mine,
　　Nor had my hopes have dar'd so soon o'er love
　　　　the victors be.
Go forth, false hearts, I curse ye not, though joy no
　　more be mine,
　　Though never, never more he's coming, coming
　　　　back to me.

THE MAIDEN'S FAREWELL.

I WILL not chide thee for the past,
    Though sore my maiden heart doth swell,
This interview shall be the last,
    And then—and *then*—False One, farewell!

If I had deem'd thou false could be,
    And ev'ry vow thou breath'd untrue;
I might not thus have wept for thee,
    Or learnt my hapless love to rue.

Farewell—farewell, and with thee take
    No blessing from my broken heart,
Although it may, for mem'ry's sake,
    Forbear to curse thee as we part.

Go! Traitor, go, and me forget;
    Go! praise the flash of beauty's eye;
Go! Leave me to my vain regret;
    To mourn—to languish—and to die.

NORTHAMPTONSHIRE LANES.

I WOULD not dwell in Southern lands,
Where Learning roves 'mid classic shrines ;
Where wavelets dance on golden strands,
And bright the eye of Beauty shines.
Though poor my purse, and low my lot,
Yet FREEDOM far too well I love,
E'er to renounce my humble cot,
And through the land of Tasso rove.
No, no ! let others praise the gleam
Of glory on Italian fanes,
My choice shall be the Poet's theme,
And England's pride—our Country Lanes.

The snowy spray of trees in Spring ;
The song of birds in summer time ;
The glitt'ring insects on the wing ;
The distant church bells' gentle chime ;
The velvet grass on which we tread ;
And Nature's fairer beauties wild :
All have a charm—not from the dead—
And breathe of pleasure undefil'd.
Far dearer than the marble halls,
Upon the warm Italian plains,
Are these bright scenes, which Labour calls
Her best belov'd—our Country Lanes.

SWEETBRIAR ROW.

SOMETIMES in our dreamings we meet with the
   gleamings
Of joys and of pleasures we never may know :
And such were my feelings—Life's secret revealings—
   When first I dar'd venture down Sweetbriar
   Row.

For there, with her mother—at sea is the brother—
   Resides a fair Maiden, the sweetest I know ;
That were I a stoic, my feelings heroic
   Would yield to the Beauty of Sweetbriar Row.

A Damsel the neatest, compactest, completest,
   The loveliest Darling on earth here below ;
Whose laughing and smiling, each sorrow beguiling,
   Makes happy the cottage in Sweetbriar Row.

I feel a strange yearning—a kind of heart-burning—
   And fain would my bachelor pleasures forego ;
For all things comparing, I'd rather be sharing
   The snug little Eden of Sweetbriar Row.

K

But, truly confessing, I fear that's a blessing
    That ne'er will be granted to me here below ;
Yet whate'er my fate is —digging gold or *potatics*—
    I'll ever think kindly of Sweetbriar Row.

May never a morrow dawn clouded with Sorrow ;
    But Peace and Contentment continually flow
In sunshiny brightness, and glad-hearted lightness,
    To bless the dear Maiden of Sweetbriar Row.

WOMAN'S PRIDE.

Let him pass me scornful by,
    What care I ?
To look as cold I can try,
    So for looks—What care I ?
The pangs I feel he shall not know ;
Nor sigh, nor tear my love shall show.

Another heart he may woo ;
    What care I ?
He may court, and wed her too,
    That he may—What care I ?
So that my grief he doth not know,
Until in death my love I show.

Then he may his error find ;
What care I ?
Wish he had not been so blind ;
Hopeless wish—What care I ?
Though peace and rest no more I know,
A broken heart his grief shall show.

WHERE THE CLUSTERED IVIES CREEP.

Where the clustered Ivies creep,
In the cold and pale moonshine,
Silent bow thy head and weep—
Oh! Lady fair, lady mine!
For paler than the moonbeam's light,
And colder than their ghostly shine,
Thy heart's Love lies where rag'd the fight
Which stain'd with blood the banks of Tyne.

Knight! I pray thee leave me now,
Here alone before the shrine,
For my Love to mourn and bow :
Oh! Darling brave, darling mine!

Why didst thou leave thy bonny home,
Thy stately keep with turrets nine,
To crimson with thy blood the foam
Which laves the banks of silver Tyne?

Lady! I have gold and land,
And they all shall aye be thine,
If I win thy lily hand,
Oh! Lady fair, lady mine!
Weep not thy Love, for false was he ;
Round other forms his arms would twine :
Far better for thy sake that he
Thus sleeps besides the banks of Tyne.

False! Sir Knight! false to thy glave,
Take thou back each word of thine :
My Love was ne'er a dastard slave ;
Oh! Darling brave, darling mine!
Untarnish'd was my true Knight's shield
No thought of evil dimm'd its shine :
My heart to thee I cannot yield,
It buried lies by gentle Tyne.

Listen, Lady! I am strong ;
Gems I have, and silks, and wine ;
They to thee shall all belong—
Oh! Lady fair, lady mine!

If not, there is a castle grim,
With cells therein where thou shalt pine,
And sob and mourn in vain for him
Who rests besides the banks of Tyne.

Back ! base wretch ! no Knight art thou,
Scorn alone from me is thine.
Look ! He stands beside thee now !
Oh ! Darling brave ! darling mine !
Now fly, thou guilty craven, fly ;
Frustrated in thy base design.
My Love still lives ! He did not die
Where flows the sweet and lovely Tyne.

AH! OFT WILL WE REMEMBER.

Ah ! oft will we remember
    The times long—long ago,
When first life's sweetest pleasure
    Our youthful hearts might know ;
As fondly we would wander,
    Thy fair hand clasp'd in mine,
Or with a joy still fonder,
    I press'd my lips to thine.

We dream'd not of the morrow—
    Its bitter pains and care—
Its heart-consuming sorrow---
    Its anguish and despair !—
When I from thee departed
    To cross the foaming main,
And left thee weary hearted
    To weep for me in vain.

They told thee I had perish'd—
    That they had seen my grave—
Yet still thou ever cherish'd
    The locket which I gave ;
And when they bow'd before thee,
    To crave thy heart and hand,
And vow'd they did adore thee -
    The fairest in the land.

Still from them turn'd thou coldly,
    Till one—a noble youth—
Did speak to thee more boldly,
    And *thou* believ'd his truth.
Again the halls were lighted,
    And shone on jewels rare ;
Again thy vows were plighted,
    And no one cried " Forbear."

They led thee to the altar,
  Nor deem'd that I was near,
Oh, how thy voice did falter !
  I still to thee was dear.
But I, unknown, returning,
  Had mingled with the crowd,
And, oh! my spirit's yearning,
  I might not—could not shroud.

There was no time to linger—
  No time—or I had seen
The ring placed on thy finger—
  A bar each heart between.
But I sprang forth and nam'd thee ;
  My arm was round thee thrown :
Old love prevail'd—I claim'd thee—
  And *now* thou art mine own.

DONATI'S COMET, 1858.

With fiery speed, it darts from distant realms
Of boundless space, where countless orbs revolve
In everlasting orbits vast ; and stars
In millions crown the universe sublime,

From where—far beyond our weak mortal ken—
Doth world succeed to world, e'er seeming near,
Though miles and miles apart, and numberless,
Aye, even as the golden grains of sand
On which the foamy waves of ocean leap.

The Earth primeval, long ere man was form'd,
Beheld its graceful curving form adorn
The azure firmament: and when the tribes
Of men o'er earth were spread, they gaz'd in awe
On the—to *them*—dread fearful sign of HIM,
Whose will can guide the planets in their course.
And priests would falter in their prayers, and haste
To offer up the bleeding sacrifice ;
While kings would quake with fear, cold, undefin'd ;
Yet babes would gaze and smile in innocence,
While clasp'd within their weeping mothers' arms.

The multitudes would throng the temples proud,
Of fabled gods, or senseless idols frail,
And bow them down in terror unrestrain'd,
And beat their breasts, or hopeless cry aloud,
Till nobler creeds prevailed, and science bared
The hidden secrets of the spheres, and told
How simple, yet profound, the laws which guide
Fair nature on her ceaseless march ; and prove
The far-seeing wisdom, and love divine,
Of God, the Great Eternal Architect
Of the Earth, and Heavens, and all therein.

ONWARDS.

Whene'er you love a maiden fair,
　And she receives you coldly ;
Let not her frown bid you despair,
　But, manlike, woo her boldly.
Then, should your pleadings prove in vain,
　Pine not in sadness lonely,
But seek some other heart to gain,
　And bid it love you only.
Let not your hopes be as the reed
　Which bends before the blast, Man !
The longest day—the toughest fray—
　Must surely end at last, Man !

If inward yearnings bid you rise
　From your condition, lowly,
To mingle with the Good and Wise,
　And share their mission holy :
Go fearless on, nor anger feel
　At those who stand before you :
If you but *rise*, the slaves will kneel,
　And, as a God, adore you.

The owner of a dauntless heart,
   Though poor his lot may be, Man !
E'er plays in Life the victor's part,
   And stands erect and free, Man !

In Love and Fame, 'tis aye the same,
   And will be so for ever,
The golden laurel they shall claim,
   Who *onward* still endeavour,
And upward gaze—the ill and strife
   Of mean hearts proudly scorning—
And deem the griefs and cares of life
   As night before the morning.
Then never shrink, but battle on
   Till Truth and Right prevail, Man!
The Kings of Thought their triumphs won,
   By daring NOT to *fail*, Man !

BERNARD.

SWIFT let it flash with light'ning speed
   O'er each electric wire,
That England's Saxon heart still glows
   With Freedom's quenchless fire !

That NEVER to a Despot's frown
 Her Lion Soul will yield ;
But fearless raise her arm of might,
 The poorest Exile shield !
That though a Tyrant's steel-clad serfs
 May growl across the sea,
She'll clasp her birthright to her heart,
 And dare, aye, dare be FREE !

She needs no armies, fierce and grim,
 To guard her Monarch's throne ;
But trusteth to her People's love,
 And lives in *that* alone.
She fears no Murd'rer's gleaming blade,
 Nor Revolution dark ;
But saileth o'er the troubled waves,
 Secure in Freedom's Ark.
No friend to spies, or coward plots,
 Will dear Old England be,
While panoplied with Truth and Right,
 She dares, and *will* be FREE !

Aye, even so, though kings combine
 And strive to cause her fall,
With scornful smile, erect she'll stand,
 And proud defy them all.

Sweet liberty she loves too well
  E'er once with it to part,
Aye ! sooner from her throbbing side
  The red life-blood shall start :
And sooner shall her darling ones
  In death extended be,
Than she submits to kings or slaves
  And never more be FREE !

STEPHENSON.

AROUND the doors a multitude—
  Voice hush'd, and bright eye dim—
In calm expectant silence wait
  The funeral of *him*—
Of HIM—the lowly miner's son,
  Who battled with his fate ;
And fought his way till England bade
  Him stand amidst her great.
A sudden start—the crowd falls back—
  " Throw back the portals wide : "
Frown not, ye shades of haughty kings,
  With looks of injur'd pride :

A greater king than ye we bring
　To rest within the aisle,
And shed another glory round
　The old time-honour'd pile.

Though never golden circlet deck'd
　His clear and manly brow ;
Though never jewell'd purple bade
　The thoughtless thousands bow ;
Though never title lent its charm—
　An empty charm 'tis true—
To mark the nation's meed of praise
　To *him* so justly due ;
Yet still a king 'mid giant minds
　And lofty souls he reign'd,
And not the less that warfare ne'er
　His peaceful triumphs stain'd.
No ruin'd cities mark'd his track ;
　No weeper curs'd his name :
He sought no crimson'd laurel wreath
　To cloud his well-earn'd fame.

The lofty arch, whose span unites
　The once divided shores ;
The iron path, where, night and day,
　The darting engine roars ;

The stately dock, where countless prows
 Secure in safety ride ;
The works of high and wondrous skill —
 Old England's boast and pride ;
By these alone his name shall live,
 When lesser names shall die ;
A sign of hope for failing hearts
 That doubting fear to " *try*."
Calm let him sleep by Telford's dust,
 His crown of glory won,
And bid our children tread the path
 Of ROBERT STEPHENSON.

EGYPT.

IN dreamy mood, methought I saw the banks of
 Egypt's Nile,
Where—'midst the lonely groves of palm—frown'd
 each cold massive pile ;
The ruin'd temples of an age when slaves in silence
 bow'd,
And crafty priests with gorgeous rites could awe the
 shrinking crowd

Whilst some grim Pharaoh sternly ruled,—the
    monarch of the hour—
And bade his Hebrew slaves erect his monument of
    power,
The giant record of his race ; which even now, sub-
    lime,
Swells up from Egypt's burning sands, and mocks
    the hand of Time.

What mighty changes has it seen, as there it change-
    less stood,
In calm majestic glory 'midst the Desert's solitude.
Where *now* is Egypt's wondrous lore, her science,
    and her skill ?
And where the arts with which she bow'd the nations
    to her will ?
Did e'er her proud magicians dream their altars
    would decay ;
That Egypt's pride, her strength, and pomp, would
    pass as clouds away ?
And lions prowl, and vultures creep, and slimy rep-
    tiles crawl,
Where dwelt the juggling hierophants, and sphinxes
    glared on all !

Where now are all the galleys deck'd with burnish'd
    gold and gems,
Which floated on the sacred stream like queenly
    diadems ?

And where her num'rous armies vast, which rais'd
    her o'er the lands ?

And where the ships which filled her ports, or
    nestled on her strands ?

In vain the Greek has sought to solve—aye, and the
    Roman too—

The hidden problem of the past, as each successive flew

With sword triumphant o'er the land, till super-
    stitious dread

Alarm'd their souls, and bade them flee the country
    of the dead.

The silver Queen still rules the night, the stars still
    noiseless move,

Still seasons change, and Winter's frown brings
    Summer's smile of love ;

But where are those whose intellect, and high
    aspiring mind,

In Theban halls, and Memphian stones, their death-
    less thoughts enshrin'd ?

The quaint and hieroglyphic piles to read we strive
    in vain,

As yet no mortal may unfold the secrets of the plain ;

Still this we know, and this we feel, that THOUGHT
    but seldom dies,

But ever lives in song or stone, to wake our sym-
    pathies.

THE DYING POET.

All bath'd in radiant golden light,
    The Earth in beauty lay ;
While in the west, the crimson clouds
    In glory roll'd away.
A silence reign'd with sway supreme,
    Amid the leafy woods,
Save when some feather'd songster's voice
    Rang through their solitudes.

On such an eve—through lattice green,
    Where grew the curling vine—
Above the roses sweet perfume,
    And graceful eglantine,
The zephers stole, in whispers soft,
    Towards the couch of pain,
To cool the Poet's burning brow,
    And bring him ease again.

Poor Soul ! his thoughts were with the past—
    Life's cloudless happy spring—
When first his trembling fingers touch'd
    His harp's enchanted string ;—

L

When in his dreams on Hope's broad wing
   His spirit soar'd above—
When love seem'd all the world to him,
   And all the world was love.

Ere came the change, the fatal blight,
   Of blissful Hopes destroy'd—
Ere he had learnt to mourn the wreck
   Of all he once enjoy'd.
He smiled : and then he gently laid,
   As though to sleep, his head ;
One trembling sob—one murm'ring sigh—
   And he was with the dead.

TIME TRIES ALL.

He did not smile as they did smile,
   Nor bow on bended knee ;
He did not speak as they did speak,
   In strains of flattery.
I ask'd him why he censur'd those
   Who seem'd so kind to me ?
He fix'd on me his earnest gaze—
   "*'Tis Time Tries All*," said he.

My riches fled.   My former friends
   But coldly look'd on me,
No kindly word, or gentle look,
   My heart could hear or see !
Again I met with Him I lov'd,
   I thought he too would flee :
But, no ! he clasp'd me in his arms—
   "*'Tis Time Tries All*," said he.

THE WRECK.

A REMINISCENCE OF THE ROYAL CHARTER.

IN its angry rage, loud the fierce storm roars,
   While the frost nips keen, and the rain falls fast,
As the good Ship drifts to the rock-bound shores,
   Like a child's frail toy, in the tempest blast;
And the stout hearts shrink, and the bronz'd cheeks
     pale,
   In that moment dread of bitterest gloom,
As the Storm Fiend leaps through the rifted sail,
   With a loud shrill laugh o'er his victims' doom.

From the rich gold lands of the Southern Sea,
    Had the good Ship sped o'er the dancing foam ,
And many a heart in its joy throbb'd free
    With thoughts of Country, of Love, and of Home.
And the Father clasp'd—in his dreams—his child ;
    And the Mother thought of her darling son ;
And the Maiden's face with a sweet joy smil'd
    As she mus'd of friends, or a dearer *one*.

But the pale grey beams of the cold bleak morn,
    Gleam'd sadly athwart on the corse-strewn shore,
Where the black hull lay, like a thing of scorn,
    To ride in its pride and its might no more :
Where the gold weighs down—like a red death-
      crown—
On weed-tangled brows that peacefully rest,
Undisturb'd by care, or the world's harsh frown,
    'Neath the bright white foam of the dark wave's
      crest.

While the weepers stand on the fatal strand ;
    Or silently roam o'er the wave-lash'd coast ;
With an anxious eye, and a trembling hand,
    For some relic fond of the lov'd and lost ;
To be treasur'd, oh ! with a jealous care,
    Through the long, long days, of the future drear,
Till the dreams of Life yield to visions fair,
    Of a happier Land and a brighter sphere.

CASTLES IN THE AIR.

How oft we find Life's golden dreams
   In silence disappear ;
And hearts we once could deem so true
   Prove false and insincere ;
While ev'ry bright and cherish'd hope,
   Replete with promise fair,
Dissolves as Autumn's crimson clouds—
   -Our Castles in the Air !

Alas ! the bitter truth we learn,
   As we in life proceed,
That those who trust in *words*, but lean
   Upon a broken reed :
That each fond wish—each treasur'd aim—
   And all our toil and care,
In spite of all our tears and pain,
   Prove Castles in the Air !

Turn where we will, 'tis e'er the same,
   Though rank be low or high—
The Monarch proud, the Toiler poor,
   View all their joys pass by ;

One would renounce his pomp and state
 For Labour's simple fare ;
The Toiler fain would be a Lord ;
 Oh ! Castles in the Air !

"LIVE, STILL LIVE FOR ME."

ALTHOUGH the shades of grief surround
 My youthful soul with care ;
Resign'd and calm shall it be found,
 Unting'd by wan despair.
The cloud may show its darkest side,
 The night its deepest gloom,
And each bright hope for which I sigh'd,
 Have met Life's changeless doom ;
But still my brow shall never show
 That Grief can victor be,
If thou—Dear Love—thy words will prove,
 And live, still live for me !

Let summer friends in haste depart,
 When rumour breathes of ill,
Thy smile shall cheer and soothe my heart,
 And make it happier still ;

Let fame and fortune pass away
    And leave me weak and poor ;
Let every chance in Life decay,
    To be reviv'd no more :
Yet still my brow shall never show
    That Grief can victor be,
If thou—Dear Love—thy words will prove,
    And live, still live for me.

FRANKLIN.

Where frown the snowy Arctic shores,
    Upon the frozen Main ;
Where seldom Man has dar'd to tread,
    And home return again ;
Where never grass, nor shrub, nor tree,
    Relieves the dreary gloom ;
And Upas chills from Ice-lands white,
    Through giant mist-wreath's loom :

There Franklin sleeps.   Aye! with his band
    Who fearless ventur'd forth,
From Love and Home, to seek and dare
    The dangers of the North ;

To solve the problem, dark and dread,
　　Which *we* may never know,
Of seas where canvass may not spread,
　　Or float the slim canoe.

God rest their souls!　What bitter pangs
　　For those they left behind
They must have felt ; what vain regrets
　　Have worn each drooping mind,
As, day by day, they struggled on
　　To fall, to faint, and die,
Surrounded by the sheets of snow—
　　Their dirge, the tempest's sigh.

The icy berg—the shifting floe—
　　The unknown fearful sea—
The endless plains of Sea and Snow—
　　Their monument shall be.
Long will they live the mem'ries stern
　　Of that grim spectral shore ;
Of those for whom their country weeps—
　　Whom we may see no more.

ITALY!

A Prophecy; written and printed in 1855.

Alas! for Thee, Poor Italy!
  The curse is on thy brow;
Thy Temples, and thy Palaces
  Lie desolated now!

Oh! sad and mournful is the fate
  Which Time hath brought to Thee—
Whose wide dominion was the World,
  Whose boundary, the Sea!

But yet thy great and noble acts—
  Though buried in the Past—
Around thy name and destiny,
  A flick'ring splendour cast.

And who shall dare forbid the hope
  That Thou again may rise,
To live in Glory, Fame, and Strength,
  And by the Past made wise?

Lo ! in the NORTH,* all radiant shines
　　The advent of the dawn,
When Thou shalt dash thy chains aside,
　　And laugh thy foes to scorn !

When olives rich shall glad thy fields
　　With smiles of Peace and Love ;
When joy shall tune thy Daughters' songs,
　　As through thy vines they rove :

When Babes shall lisp, and dance, and play,
　　Upon each Mother's knee ;
And Thou shalt feel the glorious bliss
　　Of Freedom's Jubilee.

MARY.

　　"NAY, William, stay "—Poor Mary cried—
　　　　" Depart not thus from me ;
Thou art far safer by my side,
　　Than on the foamy sea."

* Sardinia.

In vain she falt'ring breathes the words ;
　　He hears not prayer or wail,
For o'er the waves the LILY glides
　　With stretch'd and flowing sail.

Far, far away o'er Ocean's breast,
　　Away where breakers roar,
And crested waves in fury dash
　　Against the rocky shore :

Till manly brows are pale with fear,
　　And hearts are still with dread ;
As thunders roll, and lightnings flash,
　　Among the sails o'erhead.

Two Summers fair have grac'd the earth,
　　Since William bade farewell
To her who won his sailor heart
　　With Love's own witching spell.

Upon the Lily's deck he stands,
　　And dreams of love and home ;
Too slow for him tho good ship cleaves
　　Aside the ocean foam.

"Swift, swift, my bark, before the winds
　　With arrowy fleetness fly ;
Till thou dost rest in England's port
　　Beneath an English sky."

" See, see the distant dark'ning streak
    Above the ocean line ;
Joy, joy, my soul, it is the land—
    The bonny land of mine "

The port is reach'd, and William springs
    With haste on to the shore ;
" A post chaise, quick "—away he rides
    To meet his love once more.

" Quick, quick, my boy, your whip and spurs
    Spare not, nor use in vain
Till in these arms I fondly clasp
    My Mary's form again."

Through village old, through busy town,
    The steeds drive madly on,
The distant spire becomes more near
    Till William's home is won.

He hastens to the ancient porch,
    All—all was silent there—
An icy coldness numb'd his heart—
    To breathe he scarce could dare.

An unknown terror fill'd his breast,
    With fear he scarce could stand,
But ope'd the well-known cottage door,
    With cold and trembling hand.

A step,—a rush—a kiss—and then
   A word of fondness warm—
Ah ! wretched man, why starts he back ?
   He clasps a *lifeless* form !

THE DESERTED.

GAZE, Herbert, gaze on this wan face
That once to thee could seem so fair ;
Each smile is flown—each simple grace—
Which thou didst say wert ling'ring there ;
Yet, in its sadness, thou may'st trace
Forgiveness 'midst its lines of care.

Oft I recall'd, with moisten'd eyes,
How thou my hand first softly press'd ;
And sought an answer to thy sighs,
As thou didst clasp me to thy breast :
With thee I shar'd Love's sympathies—
In *thy* affection rapt and blest.

Oh ! hast thou e'er, at midnight hour,
Remember'd me, in silent thought,
Or felt Remorse, with stinging power,
Upbraid thee that thou idly sought
To crush the weak and helpless flower—
To blast the hopes with promise fraught !

See, Herbert, see thy gift to me—
This simple golden locket rare—
Sad pledge of thine inconstancy,
Lone witness of my wild despair ;
When—lost to Love, to Hope, and Thee—
I scarce the pangs of life could bear.

Long, long have I my fault aton'd,
Deserted by the world and *thee* !
By father, mother, all, disown'd,
No peace or rest was left to me :
In vain I pray'd, and wept, and moan'd,
No comfort sweet my heart could see.

Each lonely night, in this poor room,
I've watch'd the ling'ring moments fly ;
And long'd to lay me in the tomb,—
Death's refuge from each tear and sigh—
Nor all its awe, its chillsome gloom
Could e'er dispel the wish to die.

For oft I dreamt of that bright land,
Far, far from these domains of woe,
Where angels in their glory stand ;
Where hearts no more may anguish know ;
And e'er I long'd to reach its strand,
And to my Lord for mercy go.

Farewell—a darkness veils my eyes,
Thy kneeling form no more I see ;
Yet I forgive thee, e'en as I
Hope that my Lord will pardon me.
Farewell—I rise—I mount—I fly—
From ev'ry earthly trammel free.

FALLEN !

Oh ! beautiful and innocent
 Was her young soul within :
No taint defil'd its purity ;
 Her heart was free from sin.

No brighter worth was e'er enshrin'd
 In Poet's teeming brain ;
Oh ! that her maiden holiness
 Could be restored again.

The Tempter came.   With words of guile
    He led her heart astray ;
Her guardian angel spread her wings,
    And, weeping, flew away.

The Tempter won—His victim fell—
    And *now* in grief and pain
Her spirit agoniz'd recalls
    Life's early days again.

ROSALIND.

For thee no brazen trumpets blow,
For thee, no silken banners wind,
Yet thou art ever in the heart
Of haughty Strathclyde's Rosalind.
Aye ! dearer thou than belted Earl,
Or Prince with all his vassal train ;
I care not for thy lowly birth,
But loving, am belov'd again.

The Monarch's crown of peerless worth,
Though it may bid ambition start,
Can never yield the smiles of joy
Unless shared with some faithful heart ;

And I would rather be with thee,
Than wear Rank's trappings false and vain ;
The heart alone shall be my guide,
For, loving, I am lov'd again.

For thee my fortune I resign ;
For thee, I rank and all forego ;
For thee, I leave my father's halls
To share thy future weal or woe.
A simple cottage in the vale,
Shall hear my voice echo the strain
Of how I left my castle home,
To love, and be belov'd again.

HUBERT.

On ! mother, mother, do not weep for thy poor
  dying boy,
Nor blame the hand which thus deprives thy heart
  of all its joy ;
For never since that fatal eve when *she* was lost to
  me,
My soul has known one hour of rest, from pain or
  anguish free.

I could not pass the meadow path, or wander through
    the grove,
But ev'ry flower and ev'ry tree recall'd my days of
    love ;
On Sabbath days, the church-yard old with trembling
    feet I trod,
And, weeping, monrn'd the loss of her who lay be-
    neath the sod.

I ever saw her in my dreams, in all **my** silent woe!
I see her now—she smiles on me—nay, do not
    tremble so—
A calmness glides across my heart—no more its
    feelings swell,
My life is ebbing—kiss me now—I go—mother,
    farewell !

THE TIFF.

You had better go away, John,
    Nor for my love implore,
For I your sweetheart will not be,
    So trouble me no more.

What is the use of talking thus ?
   I will not walk with you ;
Now, John, be off, you hinder me,—
   Indeed, I'm sure you do.

You had better go away, John,
   You really bore me quite ;
Dont tell me I am " beautiful "—
   That I'm your soul's " delight."
Provoking 'tis, I do declare,
   That me you torment yet ;
I'm sure that such a swain as you,
   No damsel yet has met.

You had better go away, John ;
   Ah ! what is that you say—
That you " will take me at my word,
   And walk with Fanny Grey."
You cannot be in earnest, John,
   To leave me all alone ;
Why dont you know I love but you ?—
   You are my darling, John.

Oh ! go not then away, John,
   My error I confess,
My heart is yours, and you, I trust,
   Will love it none the less,

Because I cast the mask aside,
   And bared my maiden heart,
That you might know my secret thoughts,
   Nor from me cold depart.

THE COURSE OF TRUE LOVE NEVER
RUNS SMOOTH.

On ! there's a young man comes courting poor me,
By night or by day he will not let me be ;
'Tis in vain that I frown, look solemn and glum,
Or keep my mouth just as if I was dumb ;
For 'tis all of no use, he wont let me be,
But always is coming, and bothering me.
      Oh ! dear ; oh ! dear ; I wish he would go,
      A troublesome man shall ne'er be my beau.

If I go to the church, or go to the fair,
'Tis a thousand to one that he will be there ;
And if I leave home for a stroll in the street,
The tiresome fellow I'm certain to meet ;

While if in the house I should happen to be,
He always is coming, and bothering me.
      Oh! dear, oh! dear, I wish he would go.
      A troublesome man shall ne'er be my beau.

He says that he loves me, perhaps it is true,
But then, with the matter, I've nothing to do ;
I'm very well pleas'd with my single life,
And should I get tired I *wont* be his wife ;
Still 'tis all of no use, he can't let me be,
But always is coming and bothering me.
      Oh! dear, oh! dear, I wish he would go,
      A troublesome man shall ne'er be my beau.

Yet, if he's in earnest, perhaps I might try
To see if my heart will for ever deny
His prayers, and his wishes ; for really I'm sure,
There's some evils exist which we must endure ;
And if I dont have him, he'll ne'er let me be,
But'll always be coming and bothering me.
      Oh! dear, oh! dear, I wish I could know
      How to get rid of this troublesome beau.

THE CHILD AND THE VIOLET.

Once a fair hair'd child, in the woodlands wild,
   Carelessly roam'd through Nature's bowers ;
With joy infantine his hands would he twine,
   And thoughtless pluck her fairest flowers.

Gay Daffodils he—with a childish glee—
   In gay wreaths bound around his brow,
With the Daisy white, and the Crocus bright,
   Nor mark'd their forms in sadness bow.

Still onward he went, with his mind intent
   On gath'ring all that he might view—
Star of Bethlehem, and the woodland's gem—
   The lovely, dreamy Violet blue.

And soon did he find, 'mid the green leaves shrin'd—
   Where hedgerow trees, with shelt'ring care,
Forth their broad arms cast, from the fierce north
     blast,
   To shield its tiny blossoms fair—

The pride of the grove ; the flower of our love ;
   The purple princess of the woods,
Whose modesty shames the airs of our dames,
   Who flaunt their charms in vainest moods.

The child's sparkling eyes, at sight of the prize,
    Beam'd with a lustre, radiant, bright ;
And his soft cheek glow'd with a flush that show'd
    His heart's rich fulness of delight.

Forth he gaily sprang, with a cry that rang
    Like music through the long groves lone,
Where the timid hares peep'd forth from their lairs,
    Or crouch'd behind some moss-clad stone.

When suddenly down fell his flow'ret crown,
    Wither'd and dead, its young strength gone,
Like the dreams of life that sink 'neath the strife
    Of worldly warfare, hate, and scorn.

With a backward start, and a falt'ring heart,
    The child withdrew his spoiling hand ;
And then with the glance of a soul-wrapt trance
    The dying buds he slowly scann'd.

Till the violet fair, with its fragrance rare,
    Did seem to crave his pitying love ;
As though with a charm it fain would disarm
    The infant monarch of the grove.

And the spring's fond flower, with a mystic power,
    His young heart rul'd with strange wild sway
As he, bending down o'er his faded crown,
    The glist'ning dewdrops kiss'd away.

And e'en as his lips touch'd the purple tips,
    The laughing fays all dancing sprang
From beneath the blades in the long green glades
    Where ne'er the stroke of axe had rang,

They danced, and they leapt ; and in and out crept ;
    In their frolicsome elfin sport ;
While the fairies bright, in their robes of light,
    The young child led to th' Elf-king's court.

And a thousand sights, rich joys, and delights,
    They brought for his glad heart to share :
With music and song they fondled him long,
    And smooth'd his silk-like golden hair.

Till a soft calm sleep seem'd to gently creep
    O'er his eyes that were wearied sore ;
Then the grateful things, on their thin gauze wings,
    Homeward the child in safety bore.

THE LAST APPEAL.

Pray, do not come to court me, Ralph,
    Your wooing is in vain ;
For though I know and feel your worth,
    My heart you ne'er will gain.

I fain would love you if I *could*,—
   To do so I have tried—
But though your friendship I esteem,
   I may not be your bride.
Nay, Ralph, why should you look so sad?
   Why should you thus despair?
In England there are maidens yet
   Whose hearts for you may care.

And you may find one to your mind,
   To share your fate in life;
To bless you in the moments dark
   Of trouble, and of strife.
I know your heart is kind and good,
   Your nature noble too,
And that each vow your lips may breathe
   Will—like yourself—be true;
But, Ralph, I cannot bid you *hope*,—
   Nay, do not tremble so,
'Tis better you should know the truth,
   Than wake to future woe.

For you, Poor Ralph, I truly feel,
   Yet I nought else can do;
To have the *hand* without the *heart*
   Would anguish bring to you.

I know the pang is hard to bear,
    But, Ralph, pray do not grieve ;
'Tis better I should speak the truth
    Than your fond soul deceive.
The cloud will swiftly pass away,
    The sorrow cease to swell—
And you will find another heart
    To love, and love you well.

"MOURN, MEN OF ISRAEL."

Mourn, Israel, mourn! for the Spoiler hath come
And this day beholds thy last look on thy home:
The glories of Zion no more shalt thou see,
For, ere the day wanes, thou a captive shalt be!

Oh! woe, woe to the hour, when in thy fell pride,
The God of thy Fathers thou spurn'd and defied;
For the wild rolling wave of Egypt's dark sea
Shall not pant more vainly or helpless than thee.

The shade of the Cypress—the chill of the Tomb,
Shall not be more dark, or more cold than the gloom
Which the pangs of despair shall cast around thee
When, a slave, thou shalt kneel and sigh to be free!

Long, long shalt thou languish, unable to save
The land of thy Monarchs from foot fall of slave,
Till Jehovah's wrath shall away pass from thee,
And thou from thy fetters art ransom'd and free.

THE CAROL SINGERS.

The cheerful fire, with ruddy glow,
　　Shone through the windows low and dim
As, cold and homeless, in the snow,
　　Two children sang a Christmas Hymn.
Amid the noise of pealing chimes,
　　Amid the harmony and mirth,
They sang how in the olden times,
　　A Child brought down goodwill to earth.

How lonely shepherds in the plains,
　　Heard angel choirs with rapture sing
The ever sweet and welcome strains
　　Of honour to the new bore King !
How came the Magi from afar,
　　With golden gift and costly gem ;
To bow before the rising star,
　　And hail the babe of Bethlehem.

As thus the children plaintive sung
　　The humble carol's simple tune ;
Their voices touch'd a heart unstrung
　　With care and grief in life too soon.—

A Mother mourn'd her darling ones,
   Who, faithful to their Country's call,
Had brav'd the foeman's hostile guns,
   And dar'd in Freedom's fight to fall.

One clove his path up Alma's height,
   Through each dread line of steel and flame ;
In Balaclava's hero fight,
   He death preferr'd to flight and shame.
His sire pac'd through the trenches damp
   In watchings for the coming fray;
For oft the Russ, with stealthy tramp,
   Would strive by craft to gain the day.

At last there came a random shot
   Which pierc'd the father's lion breast ;
His comrades rush'd towards the spot—
   Too late ! His soul in death did rest.
Such was their fate—the sire and son.
   For England's cause, for love, and right,
They Freedom's battles nobly won,
   And help'd the foeman's strength to smite.

Alas ! that War should even now
   Stalk forth with hands all bloody red,
Through India's clime, where thousands bow
   In tears and sorrow for the dead.

Oh! that the time arrived would be
　　When Strife and War should ever cease—
When, leagued in love and amity,
　　Mankind should hail the Prince of Peace!

THE SOLDIER OF THE CROSS.

He did not die 'mid War and Strife,
　　Upon the blood-stain'd field,
Where bleeding forms—with curse and oath—
　　To God their spirits yield!
He did not die like Earth's proud kings,
　　'Mid regal pomp and state :
Death's angel clasp'd him 'neath his wings,
　　And bore him to the gate
Of those bright realms beyond the sky—
　　The Martyr's blissful home ;
Where never sorrow, tear, nor sigh,
　　Within its bounds may come.

He bravely fought, but not in aid
　　Of proud and turban'd Turk ;
His battle fields were courts and lanes,
　　Where vice and fever lurk !

To feed the hungry, aid the poor ;
 Redeem outcasts from shame ;
He gave his *all*, and yet the world
 Scarce knows his humble name :
But He who rules the starry spheres,
 And frames our mortal dust,
Will place him on His own right hand,
 With love and wisdom just.

PEACE.

If fell ambition would but cease
 To sway the hearts of Kings,
We then might dare to hope and wait
 For brighter, happier things :
The weeping lands, that bleeding mourn
 The curse of factious strife,
Would welcome Peace with smiling joy,
 And leap anew to life.

For oh ! we dearly love the joys
 Which she alone canst bring ;
And, for her sake, the warrior's sword
 We dare from us to fling.

Then linger not, dear Peace, but come
　And social love restore,
Among the nations of the earth,
　And bid them war no more.

DYING.

FAREWELL! The thought I cannot brook
　That thou from me will soon be gone;
That I on thee no more shalt look,
　But lone and weeping for thee mourn.
I view thy cold and glassy eye;
　I see thy pale and bloodless cheek;
And hear thy low and feeble sigh,
　Which breathes the prayer thou canst not speak.
FAREWELL! Thy gentle spirit soon
　Will enter Heaven's bright domain;—
Belov'd of God—Oh! precious boon—
　Cheap purchas'd with a life of pain.
Within the gloomy borderland
　Of Death, thy soul has tarried long,
Impatient with the blest to stand—
　To join the Angels' choral song:

And thou hast seen, with sweet delight,
  The visions of thy future home,
Where forms celestial, cloth'd in white,
  E'er bid thee haste, and to them come.
FAREWELL!   Again I breathe the word
  Which bids my eyes with tears to swell—
Which rends again the spirit sear'd,
  That scarce can breathe the word—" *Farewell*,"
Until the restless hand of Time
  Shall bring the common doom to me ;
And waft my soul, with joy sublime,
  To Heaven, Hope, Repose, and Thee.

BRIGHTER DAYS.

WHEN the ties of Life are broken,
And those we love from us depart ;
When the fatal words are spoken,
Which fall in sadness on the heart :
Then, the anguish of our sorrow
We feel in all its bitter woe ;
Hopeless of the brighter morrow,
When tears and sighs we shall not know.

N

As the silent stars prevailing
O'er clouds of dark and sombre hue ;
So shall end our grief and wailing,
If we to each will be but true.
After storms, the sunbeams starting,
Shed rich refulgence o'er the plain ;
Thus the sorrows of our parting
Shall we forget, and meet again.

WHAT WE MIGHT HAVE DONE.

In Youth we start with brave resolves
    To win a rare and lofty name—
To be enroll'd amid the few
    Who have secur'd the crown of fame.
But when our brows with age are grey—
    When Life's brief course is all but run—
Each restless soul, with weary sigh,
    Will muse on what it *might* have done.

All dark and drear the Past will seem,
    Wherein the loss outweighs the gain ;
The idle, empty, passing dream
    Of moments objectless and vain :

And ev'ry laurel we have claim'd,
　　Each high achievement we have won ;
But cause the soul to bend and mourn,—
　　To weep for what it *might* have done !

The precious time to Folly thrown,
　　The hours to Self indulgence lent,
The many days in useless sighs
　　And coward lamentations spent—
If used aright with cheerful zeal,
　　Would calm our hearts till life had run ;—
Would help us win the glory-crown,
　　Nor mourn for what we *might* have done !

"SHOULD THOU BY FORTUNE BE CAST DOWN."

SHOULD thou by fortune be cast down,
　　Yet brave resolve to rise again ;
To strive, and win the joys which crown
　　Our earthly pilgrimage of pain.

Go fearless on, nor list to those
   Who from thy path to turn thee try ;
Who tell thee " Life is but despair,"
   Believe them not, for 'tis a lie.

When Ignorance at knowledge rails,
   And says—" 'Tis folly to be wise ; "
That lore scholastic ne'er prevails,
   But from the light of Reason flies ;
When Bigots say that we were made
   To live, to suffer, and to die,
Without one joy or earthly bliss :
   Out on them all, they do but lie !

When grave debaters, cold and proud,
   E'er strive, with faction's aid, to make
An unfair law for Labour's crowd,
   Another for the rich man's sake ;
And when reprov'd with being unjust,
   Declare it is in vain to try
The law of kindness with the poor :
   Out on them all, they do but lie !

When despots prate of right divine ;
   When statesmen plead for selfish end ;
When sophists preach that formal rites,
   Not faith and truth, their creed defend ,

When misers rail at pelf and self ;
   When mortals vow for love to die ;
When Beauty would her charms forswear ;
   Out on them all, they do but lie !

HYMNS FOR PEACE.

Written during the Russian War.

I.

GREAT Lord! thy arm of might extend,
   And bid the din of warfare cease ;
Convert each foeman to a friend—
   Opponents but in arts of peace.
The cannon's loud and angry roar—
   The bitter clash of hostile swords—
The plains where slain lie scatter'd o'er—
   The homes destroyed by ruthless hordes :
Oh ! Lord, let these no longer be
   Earth's dark disgrace, and Man's dread shame :
But let each heart incline to thee,
   And learn to bless thy holy name.

Then shall the nations, sweetly chang'd
 From strife to love's own fondest mood,
Be never more from each estrang'd,
 But flourish ever wise and good.

II

To Thee! our Saviour, Guide, and Friend,
Our knees in humbleness we bend;
And hopeful breathe the earnest prayer,
That Thou this land from strife will spare.
 By the widow's cheek so pale;
 By the orphan's bitter wail;
 By the captive's helpless fate;
 By the homes all desolate;
 By the lands, untill'd, unsown;
 By the pangs which we have known,
 For loss of father, brother, son—
 Without a prayer, to judgment gone!
 By each village, burnt and black;
 By the red and bloody track
 Of the armies, which now stand
 To curse with war each peaceful land;
We Thee implore, that Thou, thine hand
Extending o'er each hostile strand,
May stay the torrent of the war;
And cause to beam fair Mercy's star!

Lend us Thy aid that strife may cease ;
And vict'ry bring us Joy and Peace ;
Whose smiles shall cause the earth to bloom,
And swift dispel the cloud of gloom
Which shroud our hopes, and shed despair
O'er hearts that once were free from care :
Grant this, oh ! Lord ; and earth shall ring
With praise to Thee—Eternal King !
Whose word is love—whose smile is law—
Unchanging, changeless, evermore.

THE CHRISTMAS CHIMES.

Written on the occasion of the death of the Author's Mother.

HARK ! the merry chimes are pealing
    From the belfry loud and clear ;
Tear-drops down my cheeks are stealing.
    As the joyous sounds I hear.
Children are Christ's carols singing
    In the frost, and in the snow ;
Every strain my soul is bringing
    To the Comforter of Woe !

Him—whose cradle was a manger.
　　Him—who died upon the tree—
To earthly peace and joy a stranger—
　　That Mankind might all be free !

Still, my soul, with anguish smarting.
　　Yearns unto the silent dead—
Yet I feel the pang of parting
　　Ere her gentle spirit fled !
Oh ! the hands clasp'd close in sorrow,
　　Her beloved son to leave ;
Hopeful yet of the " to-morrow "
　　In the realms where none may grieve.
Oh ! the arms so fond enfolding
　　Mine to her in fond embrace ;
Whilst her blue lips, slow unfolding,
　　Breath'd of God's eternal grace.

Gone, alas ! a priceless treasure
　　Seems for ever lost to me ;
Never more my heart with pleasure
　　Will rebound, as fancy free.
Like the leaves in Autumn falling
　　From the lone and sombre groves,
Death from me is ever calling
　　All my fondest, truest loves.

Every heart-string now is riven,
   Every nerve is rack'd with pain,
Let, Oh! God, to me be given
   The repose I seek in vain.

Let not Life's severest trial
   Bow me down before my day ;—
Thou who know'st the self denial
   I endure "'neath sorrow's sway."
To Thy mercy still a stranger
   Onward do not let me go,
Through the world a hopeless ranger—
   Do not, Lord, let it be so :
But assist my weak endeavour
   To be ever truly Thine ;
From Thy way departing never
   Whilst this wayward life is mine.

THE FLIGHT OF TIME.

Revolving Time finds Mankind chang'd
   As each succeeding year fleets by —
Many a loving heart estrang'd,
   And left to linger, pine and die.

The mask torn off from Falsehood's face ;
    Transformed to friends our seeming foes ;
And those we clasp'd in Love's embrace,
    In Death's cold arms have found repose.
Many a dream has been dispell'd ;
    Many a strain has ceas'd to flow ;
And those who erst Man's homage held,
    Find fickle Fate can frowns bestow.

Oh ! could old times once more return,
    No more neglected should they be :
But, from the Past, the soul should learn
    Its thoughts from Folly's chains to free.
Alas ! we feel the flight of Time,
    With age each form begins to bend ;
Yet oft we spurn the truths sublime
    Which might to us contentment lend :
For what are crowns, or gems, or gold,
    Compar'd with promis'd joys above ;
Where bliss repays pain thousandfold,
    And for our faith yields boundless love ?

Finis.

LIST OF SUBSCRIBERS.

	COPIES.		COPIES.
The Duke of Argyll	1	Sir F. Shuckburgh, Bart....	1
The Duke of Buccleuch ...	4	Sir John Bowring, D.C.L.	1
The Duke of Devonshire ...	4	Sir David Brewster, K.H.,	1
The Marquis of Bristol	2	F.R.S.	1
The Marquis of Exeter	5	Sir J. B. Burke,	1
The Earl Brownlow	1	Sir C. D. Crosley	1
The Earl of Denbigh	2	Sir P. Fairbairn	1
The Earl of Euston	2	Sir Fitzroy Kelly, Q.C.,	
The Earl Fitzwilliam	4	M.P.	2
The Earl Spencer	10	Sir R. J. Murchison, F.R.S.	1
The Viscountess Hood	1	The Rt. Hon. Sir L. Peel...	1
Viscount Raynham, M.P.	1	Sir J. Prior	1
Viscount Campden	1	Sir E. S. Walker	1
Lord Aveland	1	Sir J. G. Wilkinson, RF..S.,	
Lord Brougham	4	D.C.L.	1
Lord Burghley, M.P.	4	Sir J. Watts	2
Lord Farnham	4	E. Baines, Esq., M.P.	1
Lord St. John	2	T. Bazley, Esq., M.P.	2
Lord St. Leonards	12	C. Buxton, Esq., M.P.	4
Lord Stanley, M.P.	1	G. Cubitt, Esq., M.P.	2
Lord Southampton	4	Grant Duff, Esq., M.P. ...	2
Lord Wharncliffe	1	J. H. Gurney. Esq., M.P....	1
Sir W. de C. Brooke, Bart.	1	R. Hanbury, Esq , M.P. ...	1
Sir E. H. L. Dryden, Bart.	2	G. W. Hunt, Esq., M.P. ...	4
Sir P. P. Duncombe, Bart.	1	W. Jackson, Esq., M.P. ...	1
Lady Duncombe	1	R. Knightley, Esq., M.P....	1
Sir C. E. Eardley, Bart. ..	1	E. A. Leatham, Esq., M.P.	1
Sir F. H. Goldsmid, Bart.,		W. N. Massey, Esq., M.P.	1
Q.C., M.P.	1	R. M. Milnes, Esq., M.P....	1
Sir B. F. Head, Bart,	2	Titus Salt, Esq., M.P.	1
Sir S. M. Peto, Bart., M.P.	2	M. D. Hill, Esq., Q.C.	1
The Rev. Sir G. S. Robinson, Bart.	2	E. F. Law, Esq., Mayor of Northampton	1

	COPIES.
Charles Knight, Esq.	2
J. Payne, Esq., Q.C.	1
Major-General Cartwright	3
C. Hughes, Esq., Clerk of the Peace, Northamptn	1
General Bouverie	4
Rev. G. E. Maunsell, Thorpe Malsor	3
Rev. Thomas James, M.A. Theddingworth	2
Rev. T. J. Bigge, M.A., Rockingham	1
Rev. T. H. Madge, M.A., Kettering	1
Rev. J. M. Simpkinson, M.A., Brington	1
Rev. W. M. H. Church. M.A., Geddington	1
Rev. C. Girdlestone, M.A.	1
Rev. T. W. Barlow, M.A., Little Bowden	1
Rev. J. Field, M.A.	1
Rev. H. V. Broughton, M.A., Wellingborough	1
Rev. G. P. Stopford, M.A., Warkton	1
Rev. L. V. Harcourt, M.A., London	1
Rev. W. Tyler, London	1
Rev. Sidney Gedge, M.A. Northampton	1
Rev. C. Isham, M.A., Lamport	1
Rev. T. W. Carr, M.A., Loddington	1
Rev. W. Law, M.A.	1
Hon. and Rev. L. Noel, M A., Exton	1

	COPIES.
Rev. A. W. Brown, M.A., Gretton	1
Rev. T. Prust, Northamptn	1
Rev. D. Morton, M.A., Rothwell,	1
Rev. R. Roberts, M.A.	1
Rev. P. H. Knight, M.A.	1
Rev. T. Drake, M.A., Barrow-on-Soar	1
Rev. D. Glover, M.A., Kingsthorpe	1
Rev. G. Capron	2
Rev. F. Tearle, M.A., Kettering	1
Rev. J. Lynes, M.A. Melchbourne	1
Rev. A. Rigg, M.A.	1
Rev. — Wilson, M.A.	2
Hon. and Rev. F. Tollemache, Harrington	1
Rev. C. Heycock	1
The Hon. Mrs. Maunsell	2
The Hon. Mrs. Watson	1
The Hon. Mrs. Sawbridge	1
The Hon. F. P. N. Vernon	1
Dr. Spencer Hall, Derby	1
The Hon. Miss Palmer	2
G. Godwin, Esq., London	2
G. Palmer, Esq.	1
H. O. Nethercote, Esq.	2
Thomas Rothwell. Esq., Manchester	2
James Hanson, Esq., Bradford	1
Dr. Mark, Manchester	2
J. F. Hollings, Esq., Lester	1
A. Macmillian, Esq., Cambridge	1

COPIES.

J. B. Baker, Esq. 1

W. Rice, Esq., Weston Flavel 1

Dr. J Watts, Manchester... 1

W. Smith, Esq., Northampn 2

J R. Portal, Esq., Northampton 1

H. H. H. Hungerford, Esq., Dingley 1

J. W. Ripley, Esq............ 1

S. Mendal, Esq. 1

R. Charlton, Esq., Bristol 1

J. W. Parker, Esq , Oxford 1

— Eland, Esq., Higham Ferrers 2

G. Burnham, Esq. 1

T Hamilton, Esq. 1

John Phillips, Esq............ 2

— Isted, Esq. 2

G. Rooke, Esq................. 1

J. Yorke, Esq., Thrapston 1

J. Woolley, Esq., Leeds ... 1

Miss L. Lewis 1

Thos. Piper, Esq , London 1

G. Smith, Esq., London ... 2

G. Plucknett, Esq., London 1

S. Andrews, Esq., London 1

Thornton Hunt, Esq., London 2

Professor Donaldson, London 2

T. E. Cliffe Leslie, Esq., London 1

F. R. Reilly, Esq., London 1

J. Plummer, Esq., London 1

Mrs. E. Thomas, London... 1

Mr. S. Plummer, London... 1

Mr G Althorp, Bradford 1

COPIES.

Mr. J. Stevenson, Northampton 1

H. Terry, Esq., Northampt 1

J. Becke, Esq , Northampton 2

H. P. Markham, Esq., Northampton 1

W. Murphy, Esq , Wellingborough 1

J. Tucker, Esq., Pavenham 2

P. McLoskey, Esq., M D., Rothwell 1

W. Dash, Esq., Kettering 1

J. Wallis, Esq., Kettering 1

J. T. Stockburn, Esq., Kettering 1

Joseph Stockburn, Esq., Kettering 1

M P. Manfield. Esq., Northampton 1

G. De Wilde, Esq., Northampton 1

R. Biddles, Esq., Kettering 1

Mrs. Leech, Kettering...... 1

Mr. H. Draper, Kettering 2

Mr. R. Haseltine, Bilston 1

Mr. F. Wallis, Kettering... 1

Mr. Hales, Kettering......... 1

Mr. J. Baker, Kettering ... 1

Mr. F. Wrigley 1

Mr. S. Marshall, London... 1

Mr. C. Mill, London 1

Mr. J. Wells, Northampton 1

Lucas, Brothers, London... 2

Mr. Drage, London 2

Mr. Hamer, Leeds 1

Mr. Lee, Leeds................. 1

Mr. Addley, Leeds 1

Mr Peebles, Kettering 1

1.

Dedicated to the Right Honourable Lord Brougham.

FREEDOM OF LABOUR:

A DEFENCE OF THE TRUE RIGHTS OF INDUSTRY.

"There lies before me a short treatise by a working man, popularly written, * * * * with a view of removing the prevalent but dangerous delusions on the subject of capital and wages, by explaining the true principles of economical science on this head. No student of that philosophy at either of the English—nay, at any of the Scotch Universities, where it is more studied—could have produced a better reasoned tract, or one showing more entire acquaintance with the principles."— LORD BROUGHAM, IN HIS SPEECH AT LIVERPOOL, ON POPULAR LITERATURE.

2.

Dedicated to the Right Honourable Lord Brougham.

STRIKES:

THEIR CAUSES, EVILS, AND RESULTS.

This work has received the decided approbation of the press, etc.

3.

Dedicated to the Members of the Building Trades.

A REPLY

TO THE "PRIZE ESSAY ON THE NINE HOURS MOVEMENT," OF THE BUILDING OPERATIVES.

" His noble friend (Earl Granville) had correctly stated the true principles affecting this question ; but he would forgive him for stating, that he had not stated them more correctly, or more distinctly, than had been done by a working man in one of the midland counties."—LORD BROUGHAM, HOUSE OF LORDS, Aug. 2, 1859.-- See TIMES, Aug. 3.

4.

Dedicated (by permission) to the Right Honourable The Earl of Shaftesbury.

THE RIGHTS OF LABOUR:

BEING AN APPEAL TO THE PEOPLE OF THE UNITED KINGDOM, AGAINST THE TYRANNY, FOLLY, AND INJUSTICE OF TRADES' UNIONS IN GENERAL.

5.

Dedicated (by permission) to the Right Honourable Lord St. Leonards.

SOME REMARKS

ON A PAMPHLET, BY J. T. DUNNING, ENTITLED "TRADES' UNIONS AND STRIKES: THEIR PHILOSORHY AND INTENTION."

AN ADDRESS

TO THE BUILDING OPERATIVES AND WORKING MEN OF THE WEST RIDING.

"I have another working man to cite, in consequence of having received this morning a document, as if the author had had a presentiment that I was about to attend a meeting of working men. I allude now to a working man who has distinguished himself, not in mechanism, but in a subject of a higher order than working men generally enter into—I mean a most excellent address, well reasoned, upon a most important subject, namely, that of strikes, referred to by Mr. Brown. Upon this subject great mistakes have been committed by some who have been setting labour against capital, as if capital were the enemy of labour. Such doctrines are apt to injure the men who put them forth far more than their employers. I allude to John Plummer, whom two years ago I had to quote for another pamphlet he wrote. This man is a working staymaker of Kettering, Northamptonshire, and he has just published an address to the working men of Yorkshire to dissuade them from any such injurious, and at times most costly, proceedings as those of setting up labour in opposition to the capital employed. (Cheers) I can only say of one of these tracts, that no man could reason the subject better, and shall say the same of the present; and I hope and trust that my old friends and constituents of Yorkshire will give a serious and calm attention to Mr. Plummer's reasoning."—Speech of Lord Brougham on the Opening of the Liverpool Free Library and Museum, Wednesday, Oct. 17th, 1860.

To be had of Thos. Waddington, Printer and Publisher, High Street, Kettering, or of the Author.